Ikigai
Kaizen
and
Hansei

THE TRIAD OF TIMELESS JAPANESE SECRETS

FORGE YOUR PATH TO ACHIEVE A LONG,
HAPPY, AND MEANINGFUL LIFE

MASTER YOUR INNER PEACE AND
GROW YOUR PERSONAL PRODUCTIVITY

Makoto Saito

Legal & Disclaimer

The information contained in this book and its contents is not
designed to replace or take the place of any form of medical or
professional advice; and is not meant to replace the need for
independent medical, financial, legal or other professional advice or
services, as may be required. The content and information in this
book have been provided for educational and entertainment
purposes only.

The content and information contained in this book have been
compiled from sources deemed reliable, and it is accurate to the best
of the Author's knowledge, information, and belief. However, the
author cannot guarantee its accuracy and validity and cannot be held
liable for any errors and/or omissions. Further, changes are
periodically made to this book as and when needed. Where
appropriate and/or necessary, you must consult a professional
(including but not limited to your doctor, attorney, financial advisor
or such other professional advisor) before using any of the suggested
remedies, techniques, or information in this book.

Upon using the contents and information contained in this book, you
agree to hold harmless the Author from and against any damages,
costs, and expenses, including any legal fees potentially resulting
from the application of any of the information provided by this book.
This disclaimer applies to any loss, damages or injury caused by the
use and application, whether directly or indirectly, of any advice or
information presented, whether for breach of contract, tort,
negligence, personal injury, criminal intent, or under any other cause
of action.

You agree to accept all risks of using the information presented
inside this book.

You agree that by continuing to read this book, where appropriate
and/or necessary, you shall consult a professional (including but not
limited to your doctor, attorney, or financial advisor or such other
advisor as needed) before using any of the suggested remedies,
techniques, or information in this book.

Thank You
for your purchase!

SCAN THIS QR CODE BELOW
to get your completely
FREE BONUS!

By following the directions you will receive a gift book
"Whispers of the Rising Sun
Myths and Spells from the Heart of Japan."

SCAN ME

This bonus is crafted to not only provide enjoyable reading but also to inspire and open new pathways in your journey.

By exploring the ancient Japanese tradition, you'll ensure a rewarding experience in cultivating a life of balance and harmony.

All this to thank you for your support!

Table of Content

Unveiling the Japanese Secret to Fulfillment and Success 9

.... 13

Discovering Your Purpose: Understanding Ikigai 14
The History and Origin of Ikigai 14
The Four Pillars of Ikigai 17
Finding Your Personal Ikigai 19
Case Studies: Real-Life Ikigai Examples 22
Exercises to Discover Your Ikigai 24

Aligning Your Career with Your Ikigai 26
Identifying Ikigai in Your Professional Life 26
Strategies for Career Transition 28
Overcoming Challenges in Career Alignment 30
Success Stories of Career Transformation 32
Practical Steps to Take Now 34

Ikigai in Daily Life and Relationships 37
Integrating Ikigai into Everyday Activities 37
Enhancing Personal Relationships with Ikigai .. 39
The Role of Community in Finding Your Ikigai . 41
Balancing Work, Life, and Passion 43
Activities to Enrich Your Daily Routine 45

Sustaining Your Ikigai 47
The Challenges of Maintaining Ikigai 47
Long-term Strategies for Ikigai Preservation 50
Ikigai and Mental Health 51
The Future of Ikigai in Your Life 53
Continuing Your Ikigai Journey 55

.... 59

The Art of Continuous Improvement: The Principles of Kaizen 60

Introduction to Kaizen and Its Origins 60
The 5 Core Elements of Kaizen 62
Kaizen in Personal Development 64
Kaizen in the Workplace: Case Studies................. 66
Daily Practices for Kaizen... 68

Setting and Achieving Goals with Kaizen 70
Breaking Down Large Goals 70
The Role of Habit Formation in Kaizen 72
Measuring Progress and Setting Milestones...... 74
Stories of Personal Achievement.............................. 76
Kaizen Goal-setting Workshop................................. 78

Kaizen for Productivity and Efficiency................................. 80
Tools and Techniques for Increasing Productivity
.... 80
Eliminating Waste in Your Daily Life and Work 82
Streamlining Processes for Better Results........... 84
Success Stories of Efficiency Improvement......... 86
Implementing Kaizen at Home and Work........... 88

Overcoming Obstacles with Kaizen 91
Identifying and Addressing Challenges................. 91
Kaizen Approach to Problem Solving..................... 93
- Maintaining Motivation and Focus 95
Learning from Failure: A Kaizen Perspective 97
Action Plan for Continuous Improvement........... 99
.... 101

The Practice of Reflection: Understanding Hansei...... 102
The Concept and Tradition of Hansei................. 102
- The Role of Self-reflection in Personal Growth
.... 104
Incorporating Hansei into Your Routine 106
Reflective Practices for Daily Life 109
Guided Hansei Sessions.. 111

Hansei for Personal and Professional Development...113
Using Hansei to Enhance Career Aspirations .. 113
Building Stronger Relationships Through
Reflection.. 116

The Impact of Hansei on Communication Skills
.... 118
Case Studies: Transformation Through Hansei
.... 121
Reflective Exercises for Development 123

Mastering Hansei for Long-term Success *125*
Advanced Techniques in Hansei............................ 125
Creating a Sustainable Practice of Reflection . 127
The Future of Hansei in Your Life.......................... 129
Sharing the Practice of Hansei with Others...... 131
Continuing the Journey of Reflection 134

Integrating Ikigai, Kaizen, and Hansei into Your Life 136
The Synergy of Ikigai, Kaizen, and Hansei for
Holistic Success.. 136
Strategies for Maintaining Balance and
Continuous Growth 138
Next Steps: Creating Your Path Forward........... 141

Unveiling

the Japanese Secret

to Fulfillment and Success

In the bustling cacophony of the modern world, finding harmony within ourselves and our surroundings seems like an elusive pursuit. With multiple roles to juggle and infinite paths to tread, we may often find ourselves feeling lost and unfulfilled. Despite external accomplishments, there remains a void—an internal longing—for a deeper sense of purpose and a more satisfying existence. If these ideas strike a chord with you, dear reader, take heart in knowing you're in good company. And, crucially, by choosing to engage with this book, you've set foot on a path that aligns with your quest.

My name is Makoto Saito, your companion on this journey to transformative personal and professional development. I have authored numerous bestsellers in the field of self-help, focusing on productivity and goal setting. Drawing from my extensive research and practical application, I have weaved the essence of three timeless Japanese concepts into this book: Ikigai, Kaizen, and Hansei. These are not just words, but philosophies—life-altering perspectives—that have the potential to bring joy, fulfillment, and success within your reach.

The idea of Ikigai has enchanted millions of people around the world; at its core, it combines our passion, mission, profession and vocation into a harmonious existence. This intersection of what you love, what you are good at, what the world needs and what you can get paid for is your Ikigai, your reason for being. But there is much more to this philosophy and its application in your personal and professional life than you might imagine. This book provides a lucid and practical approach to discovering and embracing your unique Ikigai.

Kaizen—continuous improvement—is a philosophy that revolutionized business operations, but its principles can be equally transformative on a personal level. Kaizen reminds us that progress isn't always about making leaps and bounds; it's about consistently taking small, patient steps towards your goal. Many of us underestimate the power of small changes. This book aims to correct that perspective and equip you with actionable strategies to implement the Kaizen principles in your life effectively.

While Ikigai and Kaizen enable us to set paths and commence our journey, Hansei—self-reflection—keeps us grounded along the way. Hansei is not just pondering our actions but critically reflecting on them. It pushes us to learn from our successes and failures equally, enriching our journeys with wisdom and clarity. This book will guide you towards incorporating regular Hansei into your everyday practices in a manageable and enriching manner.

Brought together, these three philosophies present a powerful framework for a more balanced, fulfilled, and successful life. The cumulative wisdom enlisted within these pages is not merely theoretical jargon, but a blueprint of adaptable techniques and real-life applications, designed to fit various aspects of your life—career, personal development, relationships, and hobbies.

My aspiration is to make this knowledge accessible, relatable, and practically applicable to you—regardless of your background or where you stand in life today.
As we embark on this exciting expedition, I hope you find the courage to explore, patience to transform, and the wisdom to appreciate the journey. Let's awaken the promise of Ikigai, unlock the power of Kaizen, and welcome the practice of Hansei into our lives. Here's to finding fulfillment, achieving success, and becoming the best version of ourselves!

Welcome to the journey of a lifetime—your lifetime.

Makoto Saito

.Ikigai

生き甲斐

Discovering Your Purpose:

Understanding Ikigai

The History and Origin of Ikigai

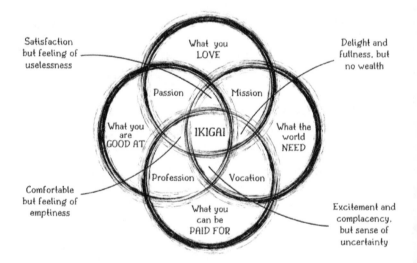

As we begin to discover the breadth of this kind of philosophy, it becomes essential to dig into its origins and understand its history. The term "Ikigai" comes from the ancient Japanese language, where "iki" means "life" and "gai" means "value," thus translating to "reason for being" or "value in life.

Ikigai is not a recent coinage or a trending self-help term. It's a philosophy deeply rooted in Japanese culture. Unearthing the roots of the term takes us back to the Heian period (794–1185), one of the most significant periods in Japanese literature when the term 'Gai' was first used in The Pillow Book by Sei Shonagon. This philosophical term further evolved during the Edo period (1603–1867), when 'Ikigai' was recognized in Japanese writings.

However, Ikigai didn't receive global attention until the late 20th century. Analyses of the healthiest and longest-living populations started gaining traction, presenting intriguing insights. The island of Okinawa, Japan, emerged as a region boasting some of the world's oldest inhabitants, ones leading not just long, but meaningful and satisfied lives.

Okinawans often attribute their longevity to their Ikigai. Famed for their high life expectancy, Okinawans are found to have a strong sense of purpose—a clear reason for waking every day. They claim this life value keeps them vibrant, motivated, and contributes to their long lifespan. Their culture doesn't revere retirement much; instead, Okinawans stay active and engrossed in their Ikigai well into old age. This insight triggered a greater exploration into the concept.

In the 21st century, authors Hector Garcia and Francese Miralles made the term known worldwide with their book "Ikigai: *The Japanese Secret to a Long and Happy Life*." Their work highlighted how finding and pursuing Ikigai can significantly improve life satisfaction, personal fulfillment and overall health.

Underlying this concept are four basic pillars, known as the four elements of Ikigai: what we love, what the world needs, what we can get paid for, and what we are good at. When these four elements intersect, they form a person's Ikigai. It allows us to delineate our passion, mission, profession and vocation, leading us to our unique "reason for being." The rules are not ironclad; this balance continually evolves according to changing life stages, personal developments and the world around us. The exercise is not to find a definitive answer, but to continually explore these elements, enriching our journey in its entirety. As we delve into understanding Ikigai, it is crucial to remember that it is inherently personal; in fact, it is not about following social norms or measuring ourselves against others. It is not about chasing popular dreams or making strides. It is about individual fulfillment. It is about recognizing one's aspirations, honing one's skills, and contributing meaningfully to the world, gaining satisfaction and value in doing so.

The idea of Ikigai goes beyond the concept of career choice. It is easy to misunderstand it as the "perfect job." Although a profession that fulfills all four pillars can be perceived as an ideal scenario, Ikigai can exist outside of our professional lives. For some, it may be a creative pursuit, continuous learning, a fulfilling hobby, or a beautiful intersection of personal interest and community service.

The concept of Ikigai is elegantly simple yet deeply powerful. Albeit deeply rooted in Japanese culture and philosophy, it seamlessly fits into any culture, any professional space, any personal scenario—making it a universally applicable mindset. Its history and origin give global audiences a unique lens to perceive life and fulfillment, nudging them to explore purpose, happiness, and satisfaction outside conventional norms. As we progress in this book, we will navigate specific techniques of unveiling your Ikigai and practical strategies to incorporate it into your daily life seamlessly. Here's looking forward to a meaningful, value-driven, and uniquely fulfilling journey!

The Four Pillars of Ikigai

As we delve into this realm, we begin to unveil the structural core of this enigmatic philosophy: The famous "four pillars." Each pillar is distinct but converges elegantly at the heart of Ikigai. These pillars are what you love, what the world needs, what you can get paid for, and what you are good at. Together, they represent the critical areas of self-discovery and self-realization, forming your reason for being.

The first pillar, "What you love," points towards the passions that light up your heart. These could be activities, experiences, or pursuits that genuinely excite you, bring a spark to your eye, and naturally, pull your interest. These passions are devoid of external validation, not dictated by societal norms or trends, but singularly hinged on your joy. Whether it be painting, gardening, teaching, entrepreneurship or anything that makes you lose track of time, the first pillar invites you to delve into those activities and ignite your intrinsic interests.

The second pillar, "What the world needs," seeks a broader perspective. This pillar highlights the understanding of our place within the greater whole, and how our passions and abilities can serve others, nourishing our communal fabric. It is about identifying areas where you can contribute positively and meaningfully to society. This could be something as big as solving a global issue or as simple as brightening someone's day. The critical aspect here is the awareness of our interconnectedness and the aspiration to influence positively.

Next, we approach the third pillar, "What you can be

paid for." Given the practical world we inhabit, recognizing what our skills, knowledge, and passions can render as a profession or vocation is indispensable. This pillar delves into understanding the marketplace, identifying opportunities that align with your abilities and interests, and creating financial stability and growth. Recognizing this pillar does not negate the idea of Ikigai being beyond a career choice; instead, it acknowledges the reality of socio-economic factors in our pursuit of fulfillment and balance.

Our final pillar, "What you're good at," pushes us to undertake a self-appraisal of our abilities. What skills do you possess? What areas are you innately proficient in? What tasks do you perform effortlessly, and what skills have you mastered over time? This pillar urges you to explore and acknowledge your talents, igniting a path of continual learning and personal growth.

These four pillars, while distinct, are beautifully interconnected. At various junctures of our life, we might find ourselves exploring these pillars separately, perhaps mastering one before we venture to the other. There may be times when finding a meeting point of all four might seem like a distant dream, yet progress lies in the journey—and every step towards uncovering these pillars brings you closer to your Ikigai.

Understand that the intersection of these four pillars is not in a fixed place, but a moving point. As you evolve, your Ikigai also evolves. Embracing this dynamic philosophy does not confine you to a single path, but opens up avenues for continual discovery and exploration. Your identity is as unique as you are, and it manifests in many forms and nuances at different stages of life.

In the chapters ahead, we will discuss practical exercises, real-life case studies, and strategies to explore these pillars effectually, leading you towards your unique Ikigai, and with it, a fulfilling and balanced life. The journey might be intricate and challenging, but the destination—a life rich with purpose, satisfaction, and accomplishment—is well worth the expedition. So let's delve deeper, culminating in a life that is uniquely and utterly yours, a life built on the fundamentals of your own Ikigai.

Finding Your Personal Ikigai

We've now ushered into an even more exciting facet of our journey—the quest of finding your personal Ikigai. As you've discovered so far, Ikigai is a deeply personal concept, a unique intersection of passion, need, profession, and ability that differs from person to person. Identifying your own Ikigai is an exploration, not a destination—an ongoing process of self-reflection and discovery.

Beginning your journey towards finding your Ikigai requires you to take an introspective dive into your life. Often, in the hectic pace of our daily activities, we overlook the need to stop and recognize what genuinely connects with our deepest values and desires. What are those activities that you could lose hours to and still wouldn't consider it time lost? What interests or hobbies ignite you, lending a spark to your eyes? Truly delve into what you love, even jotting down these passions, no matter how small or big they might seem.

Next, gaze at the world around you—the society you dwell within, the world you share with others. Where does it need assistance or service? Is there a lack you can identify: in your community, in your company, in the world at large? Are there environmental issues that concern you, social issues that impassion you, or simply an everyday problem that you have a potent solution for? This mindful contemplation generates awareness of the needs you can fulfill, carving the path for "what the world needs."

Navigating further, assess your professional abilities. Where does your competence lie? What skills or knowledge have you amassed that can be financially rewarded? This exploration can stretch beyond your current profession—it could be a talent you solely indulge in your free time, a hobby you're proficient at or a unique skill that required honing but has potential for monetary growth.

Lastly, and maybe the most challenging one, you are to discover what you are good at. Oftentimes, we fail to see our own expertise or talents, thinking of them as 'ordinary.' But every extraordinary skill began at an ordinary level, so don't discourage yourself. Instead, think about activities where you effortlessly excel—where feedback or comments have fueled your self-confidence. Also, think about tasks that you get absorbed in, where you lose track of time—that often signal innate talent and enjoyment.

Each pillar is like a compass, guiding you towards the intersection where your Ikigai resides. As the process continues, you may find fascinating overlaps and strange contradictions. You may hit roadblocks, questioning your pursuits or doubting your skills. This is natural. Remember, finding your Ikigai isn't an overnight voyage but a journey taken step by step, introspection by introspection.

Try not to rush the process or press for immediate results. Your reason for being unfolds subtly and delicately, often when you least expect it. And sometimes, what you initially perceive as your Ikigai may evolve, reflecting changes in personal growth, societal developments or life circumstances. This dynamic nature of Ikigai is what makes it uniquely yours, continually reflecting the tapestry of your life.

While it might be tempting to follow passion alone or anchor just on what you're good at, Ikigai lies in integrating these four elements, not in isolation but in unity. That's the magic and balance of it. Your Ikigai resides at the heart of your passions, abilities, income stream, and the impact you can make. So, don't discourage if your current passion does not align with your profession or if what you're good at isn't what the world needs. Keep exploring, evolving, growing.

In the journey to uncover your Ikigai, remember to be patient with yourself, to nurture your curiosity, and to stay open to possibilities. Ascertain what makes your heart happy, your mind active, and your soul content. For in this exploration, we don't just stumble upon our Ikigai; we learn to live a life of joy, purpose, and profound satisfaction—a life that's uniquely ours and fulfilling at the core.

Case Studies: Real-Life Ikigai Examples

To illustrate the concept of Ikigai, let us look at some real-life examples. The case studies, each unique, show how different individuals found their reason for being and the transformational journey each took.

Our first case brings us to Mary, a high school teacher in her late thirties. Mary deeply loved poetry and had a natural talent for it. However, her professional life didn't involve her passion for literature, as she taught physics, not English. Mary often found herself discontented, feeling a void despite a successful career. In her quest for Ikigai, Mary realized she could combine her love for poetry, her talent for it, and her skill as an educator to introduce a poetry club in her school. This venture not only allowed her to explore her passion but also fulfilled a cultural need within the student community. Following the success of her poetry club, she started including elements of physics in her poetry—bridging the gap between her profession and passion. Mary's Ikigai, thus, radiated from combining her passion, skills, the world's need, and her profession.

The second case revolves around Jonah, a software engineer in his mid-forties. Jonah had a knack for painting, which he pursued passionately during his free time. In his Ikigai exploration, he realized he could combine his profession—a skill he was paid for and was good at—with his love for art. Jonah launched a project within his company to create aesthetically pleasing user interfaces. His artwork started reflecting in his professional work, introducing creative elements to technical software, which the industry lacked. He found a niche market, his interface designs were recognized in the tech and art world, and he started getting paid commissions. Jonah's Ikigai emerged from an unexpected mixing pot of his passion, skill, profession, and a need he identified in the world.

Finally, let's look at Alice, a retired banker in her late sixties. Alice found herself lost post-retirement. While she loved gardening and was good at it, she didn't see how it could be her Ikigai. In her pursuit, she discovered her community lacked green spaces. Alice decided to put her financial acumen to use and secured funding for a community garden. She taught gardening classes, propagating her love for plants while fulfilling a communal need. Alice's Ikigai did not come from her primary profession or something she could technically be "paid for". Instead, she went on to create a harmonious amalgamation of what she loved, what she was good at, and what her community needed—emphasizing that Ikigai can be found post-retirement as well.

These case studies provide a perspective on the diverse forms Ikigai can take, and each person's journey will be distinct. You might resonate with one of these cases, or your path may look entirely different. These narratives illustrate the common thread binding every quest for Ikigai—a pursuit that transcends conventional standards of success and productivity, delving into a personal synergy of passion, need, profession, and skill.

Remember that each of these individuals has embarked on his or her own journey, faced specific challenges and found the unique form of his or her own Ikigai. Your journey, too, will encounter detours, plateaus, forks and dead ends, but as with any journey, every step forward-no matter how small-is a step toward your life essence. Embrace patience, perseverance, curiosity and joy, for the journey to Ikigai is as rewarding as the discovery.

Exercises to Discover Your Ikigai

Exploring your Ikigai goes hand in hand with conscious exercises to decipher your passions, talents, potential professions, and the needs you can fulfill in the world. Let's delve into the practical aspects of uncovering these integral components.
An essential exercise to unveil your passions is free journaling. Invest a fixed time daily to write about activities or topics that captivate your interest, inspire you, or instigate a feeling of joy. Do not censor or analyze yet; just write freely. Maintaining this practice over some time can reveal patterns and themes about what you genuinely love.

Next, identifying your unique skills demands a different exercise. Ask close friends, family, and colleagues to share their observations on what they think you excel at. This external feedback can reveal talents we often overlook. Simultaneously, engage in a self-reflection exercise, recollect instances where your efforts were fruitful, and you felt accomplished with minimal effort. Take note of these skills—they form an output, pure and innate.

Discovering what the world needs necessitates a gaze beyond personal confines. Take the time to inform yourself about local, national, global issues, community needs, or industry gaps. Engage in dialogue, be a good listener, and attend social gatherings or community meetups. Recognize patterns, recurrent issues, or shared concerns. This broad perspective will enable you to find needs aligning with your passion and skills.

Lastly, discerning what you could potentially be paid for involves market research. Identify professions, considering a demand for your skills. Keep an open mind—your analysis might lead to unconventional sources of income. For instance, if you have a knack for pottery, consider creating pottery classes or selling your creations online.

Finally, crucially, after identifying these four pillars individually, create a Venn diagram. Label these circles with your introspections of each exercise, and your Ikigai will emerge from the intersection. This visual representation helps you combine these disparate ideas and find correlations, revealing your unique essence. Remember that these exercises are not one-time tasks-they provide tools for ongoing reflection and exploration, encouraging you to evolve your being. Understanding and living your Ikigai is an ongoing process, and these exercises aim to keep it active and conscious, guiding you toward a life imbued with purpose and fulfillment.

So, pause now for a moment. Begin your first reflections; jot down your initial thoughts. There is no rush—let the process of self-discovery guide you to new insights as you continue our journey together towards unraveling your distinctive Ikigai.

Aligning Your Career with Your Ikigai

Identifying Ikigai in Your Professional Life

Let us now turn to another intriguing perspective of Ikigai: aligning your career with your being. Your professional life, where hours and hours of your daily life take place, is a significant aspect in which your essence can manifest. When your occupation is in alignment with your Ikigai, work tends to become more fulfilling and satisfying.

Identifying your Ikigai in your professional life can seem like a daunting task. You may feel that the direction of your career is not related to your passions, or you may not be sure how to find the world's need in your current professional field. But remember that this is not a matter of perfection, but rather a search for balance and fulfillment.

Consider which facets of your work bring you joy. Within your present role, there could be components that spark your interest and align with what you're passionate about. It might be the creative problem-solving, the camaraderie and collaboration during team projects, or the detailed analysis and investigation that captivates you. These are the elements of your job that overlap with 'what you love'. Further delve into 'what the world needs.' Reflect on how your professional skills can align with the needs of your workplace, community, industry, or society at large. Does the industry lack a particular skill you possess? Is there an untapped potential you can explore? Is there a project others avoid, but you are genuinely interested in?

Next, explore what you are good at. Assess your skills and talents through performance reviews, feedback from coworkers, and most importantly, personal self-reflection. In what areas do you excel? What skills come naturally to you? What tasks can you complete with relative ease?
Lastly, you're already in the domain of 'what you can be paid for' as it naturally collides with your profession. However, assessing this element involves understanding if the current spectrum of tasks you're paid for aligns with your Ikigai or whether

there's a need for a shift or an expansion of responsibilities within your professional pool.

Once you have addressed each element of your professional lens, step back and assess the situation. Draw connections, identify overlaps and gaps, recognize what aligns with your Ikigai and what moves away from it. The result will not be perfect right away. You will identify areas where your career aligns with your essence and others where the alignment blurs.

It is important to remember that perfect convergence of the four pillars in your professional life is not mandatory for Ikigai; harmony is the goal. And although the transition may seem scary, remember that Ikigai is a continuous evolution.

Perhaps the most comforting aspect of identifying one's being in professional life is the realization that it is a unique journey. Learning to view your career through the lens of Ikigai does not apply a universal formula, but instead charts a path tailored to you and your personal circumstances.

So as we delve deeper into aligning your career with Ikigai, be ready to discover and rediscover elements of your professional endeavours. Brace yourself for spotting potential shifts and changes. And most importantly, prepare to create a work environment where you feel not just productive and efficient, but also contented, balanced, and deeply fulfilled.

Strategies for Career Transition

At times, aligning your career with your Ikigai might require a career transition. This can feel daunting, and there undoubtedly will be a fair amount of uncertainty. Yet, it can be a transformative journey, steering you toward more profound fulfillment and joy in your work life. Let's explore several strategies to smoothly navigate this transition. Realize first that aligning your career with your Ikigai calls for patience and thoughtful planning. Seeing the convergence of Ikigai in your professional life may not happen overnight. Thus, an incremental approach—to take small steps towards your career transition—is often less intimidating and more manageable.

Perhaps you have a hobby that brings immense joy and one that you are skilled at? Maybe you've found a societal need that this hobby could address? Instead of a rapid transition, consider gradually integrating this into your current professional life. You might begin conducting workshops during your spare time or offering freelance services related to your hobby. Engaging in consistent self-reflection is another essential strategy. As your career transition unfolds, regularly check-in with yourself. Are you still enjoying this new path? Does it align with your Ikigai? Be ready to adjust your plan as needed, for the intersection of your Ikigai will be a dynamic space that evolves as you move forward.

Networking is a powerful tool in any career transition. Communicate your career plans and ambitions with your friends, family, professional contacts. Look for mentors in your chosen field, individuals who have walked the path you're embracing. Leverage social platforms to align with like-minded people. These connections can provide invaluable insight, encouragement, and opportunities.

Additional training or education might be required in the process of aligning your career with your Ikigai. You could be veering toward a field where your passion and the world's need intersect, but you lack the necessary skillset. Seek relevant courses, workshops, or certifications. Equip yourself with the skills and knowledge needed, readying yourself for the transition.

Lastly, allow yourself the flexibility to experiment and learn. You may need to step outside your comfort zone, try new roles or tasks, perhaps fumble and pick yourself up again. Remember: this is growth, and growth often involves discomfort. But it is this very process of trial, error, and learning that will reinforce your journey to a career aligned with your Ikigai.

Approaching a career transition armed with these strategies creates a supportive framework that navigates you through the journey. Embrace the uncertainty, acknowledge the apprehension, and remember that you're moving towards an evolving intersection—your Ikigai. And when you bring your passion, mission, profession, and vocation into harmony with your career, every advancement, no matter how small, is a badge of progress—a step towards the joyous fulfilment of living your Ikigai.

Overcoming Challenges in Career Alignment

Aligning your career with your Ikigai can be an incredibly rewarding journey. Still, it inevitably also comes with its set of challenges and obstacles. Understanding these potential hurdles and equipped with strategies to overcome them will empower you throughout your journey.

One common challenge is resistance to change.

Embarking on a new career path, especially one that significantly veers away from your current profession, can seem daunting. This fear is natural, for change often brings uncertainty and can shake up our comfort zones. To overcome this resistance, approach change incrementally. Take small steps rather than sudden, grand leaps. Even a minor change, like incorporating part of your passion into your current profession, can initiate the movement towards aligning your career with Ikigai.

Another hurdle might involve a lack of skills or knowledge required for the new career path you're envisioning. Perhaps you've identified what you love and what the world needs—but the intersection demands a skillset you do not currently possess. Confront this challenge by embracing lifelong learning. Seek out training programs, certifications, or mentorship that can equip you with necessary skills.

Maintaining economic stability during your career search can seem challenging, especially if you're transitioning from a high-paying job to a field that initially may not pay as much but aligns more with your Ikigai. Mitigate this financial fear by planning and careful resource management. Before making any career transitions, it might be beneficial to save or downsize or consider how you could create multiple income streams.

Besides, societal pressure or expectations might deter you from making a career shift, fearing judgment or misunderstanding from family, friends, or peers. To combat this, communicate openly about your pursuit of Ikigai, your goals for personal fulfillment, and alignment in your career. Surround yourself with people who support and uplift your endeavors. During this alignment process, you may encounter bouts of introspection, self-doubt, questioning your decisions or the viability of your envisioned career. Address this challenge through self-compassion. Understand that aligning your career with your Ikigai is a dynamic process, not a straight path. There's room for adjustments, trial and error, and personal growth.

Be kind to yourself throughout the journey. Remind yourself of your motivations for this transition and your aspiration for a deeper sense of fulfillment in your work life. Affirm and honor your dedication to living your Ikigai.

Overcoming these challenges may not be easy, but it is absolutely possible. And remember, these obstacles are not roadblocks, but stepping stones on your path to a career that aligns with your Ikigai—a career that enkindles your passion, utilizes your vocation, satisfies a world need and offers professional gratification. The hurdles are momentary, the transformations, permanent. Breathe and keep journeying, for the pursuit of Ikigai is an adventure of a lifetime.

Success Stories of Career Transformation

To shed some light on the enriching journey towards aligning one's career with their Ikigai, let's delve into some inspiring success stories. These narratives, drawn from real-life experiences, showcase how path-paving transitions can lead to deeper fulfillment in one's professional life.

Let's start with Lily, a successful business consultant.

Tired of incessant travels and superficial client relationships, Lily felt a profound disconnection from her job despite the attractive paycheck. On her quest for Ikigai, she realized she loved nurturing relationships and had an untapped creative flair for designing jewelry. Over two years, Lily transitioned from her consulting role, initially starting her handmade jewelry business as a side endeavor. Once she built a satisfactory income flow and saw potential in her business model, she quit her job. Today, Lily's career revolves around jewelry-making and fostering profound relationships with her clients—aligning handsomely with her Ikigai.

Next, consider Frank, a software engineer. Frank enjoyed his job but missed experiencing a tangible, positive impact on the world. Discovering his Ikigai lay in combining his technical skills with his passion for nature conservation, Frank made a massive yet gradual transition. He initiated by engaging in weekend volunteer work at a local environmental organization. His software skills proved valuable, leading to a part-time job offer where he developed environmental data tracking software. Eventually, he transitioned wholly, revamping his career identity from software engineer to a conservation technologist. His Ikigai now thrived in his professional life, blending his passion, skills, vocation, and what the world needs beautifully.

Lastly, reflect upon Laura's journey. Laura was a home-maker for several years. Though she loved budgeting and financial planning for her family, she didn't necessarily see it as something she could turn into a profession. When she stumbled upon the notion of Ikigai, she realized the need for effective financial education amongst her close-knit community. Laura began offering free financial planning workshops, which quickly gained popularity. Encouraged by her success, she received financial advisor certification, transitioning into a new career in personal finance consulting—aligning her career splendidly with her Ikigai.

These transformative narratives remind us that aligning our career with Ikigai might require embracing changes, learning new skills, and navigating uncertainties. Yet, they stand as beautiful testaments of the fulfillment, joy, and success that such career transitions can cultivate.

These stories also emphasize how personal and unique each Ikigai's path is. How you align your career with your essence will be unique. While it is essential to draw motivation from these success stories, remember not to make comparisons, but to create your own journey, a compelling story of career alignment passionately guided by your unique Ikigai.

Practical Steps to Take Now

Navigating towards a career aligned with your Ikigai is an ongoing journey, but you can start taking practical steps right now. These steps provide initial momentum, fostering a proactive approach to this transformative journey.

Firstly, start by consciously noting down elements of your current job you genuinely enjoy—the tasks that stir your passion. Is it connecting with clients? Or perhaps dissecting complex data? Recognizing elements of your passion within your current profession gets the wheels of alignment in motion.

Simultaneously, reflect on your professional potential

by identifying your unique skills in the workplace. Draw upon feedback from peers, mentors, and managers to recognize your strengths. Reflecting upon your vocation not only strengthens your self-awareness but also serves as a confidence boost while navigating the journey.

Next, invest time to educate yourself about the needs of the world, particularly within your industry or organization. Regularly engage with field-specific literature, podcasts, and seminars. Patient observation and active learning will help identify gaps you could potentially fill.

You are already engaged in what you are paid to do in your current job. The challenge is to explore how this area might expand or change to accommodate elements of your Ikigai. How might your role be improved, added to, or even slightly shifted to align in a balanced way?

Initiating bold conversations with higher-ups regarding your career aspirations can be a potent step. Express your desire to explore tasks where your passion and skills can be utilized and appreciate the world's needs. Such candid conversations can open doors for role expansion or variation.

Finally, prepare to experiment and face failures and accept them as integral parts of the process. There will be instances where your endeavours might not yield desired results. Adopt resilience and maintain consistency. Remember that the path to aligning your career with your Ikigai is not linear but a winding road with occasional bumps and roadblocks.

These straightforward actions, though simple, can spark the journey toward aligning your career with your life's purpose. As you embark on this path, keep in mind that finding your true calling is not a fixed endpoint, but an ongoing process of fine-tuning—your own unique blend, combining what you love, what the world needs, what you can be paid for, and what you are good at into a career that brings fulfillment.

Ikigai in Daily Life and Relationships

Integrating Ikigai into Everyday Activities

We have explored how Ikigai can influence and empower significant aspects of life, such as profession, however, this essence has the power to reverberate in the simplest elements of our lives. By integrating them into daily activities, we can infuse more joy, purpose and balance into every waking moment.

Start by identifying aspects of your day where you can integrate elements of your Ikigai. If you, for example, have a passion for painting, wake up half an hour early to dedicate time to this activity before work. Don't worry about creating an absolute masterpiece. What's important is diving into the pleasure of letting colors swirl across the canvas. By weaving your passion into your daily life, you begin your day in tune with one element of your life's purpose, establishing an uplifting rhythm for the hours ahead.

Next, consider tasks through the day which you're good at and ensure they are part of your routine. Maybe you have a knack for cooking. Preparing meals, rather than viewing it as a chore, can become a fulfilling experience. Relishing the process of creating delightful dishes for yourself or others can transform an everyday task into a rewarding activity infused with your special skill.

Turning attention to tasks in the realm of 'what the world needs,' look around your immediate circle. Is there a task or hobby you're good at, and your family members or roommates need? Perhaps you're great at fixing things, so take on the role of a home-quartermaster, repairing things around the house. Or maybe you have an aptitude for budgeting and can take over the role of managing monthly expenses or investments.

Finally, there may be tasks related to 'what you can be paid for,' even in your daily life. Freelancing or part-time assignments associated with your vocation or profession can be integrated into your routine, ensuring your professional skills aren't siloed away but intermingle seamlessly into your everyday life.

When we integrate elements of Ikigai into our daily activities, even the most mundane tasks become meaningful and fulfilling. We begin to live our lives more consciously, engaging in each activity-whether personal or professional-with a sense of joy, purpose and fulfillment. Our daily routine becomes a lattice of moments that resonate with the vibration of Ikigai, each action, each joy, each challenge, enriching us in subtle but profound ways. And in this lattice, as you will soon notice, each day becomes a unique record of your life lived in alignment with your essence.

Enhancing Personal Relationships with Ikigai

While Ikigai fundamentally revolves around self-discovery and personal fulfillment, it also has a profound impact on our relationships with others. In improving personal relationships, the principles of this philosophy can help promote deeper bonds, mutual understanding and harmonious coexistence.

We can apply the concept of Ikigai to our relationships by identifying those parts of our interactions that align with 'what you love.' Are there certain aspects in your relationships that bring immense joy, satisfaction, or peace? It might be that you treasure in-depth discussions with a friend until the wee hours, or you cherish the silent presence of a close one. Recognizing and nurturing these parts can help strengthen bonds that are in tune with your passions.

Next, we can consider 'what the world needs' within our personal relationships. How can you use your unique abilities to fulfill a need in your friend's, partner's, or family member's life? Perhaps a friend requires a listener, or your partner appreciates your knack for problem-solving. By meeting these needs, you naturally, and beautifully, weave your relationships into your Ikigai tapestry.

'What you are good at' brings immense value to relationships, both to you and to the people you share bonds with. Are you a good mediator, a natural cheerleader, or a reliable confidante? Recognizing and utilizing your innate abilities in your interactions boosts your self-esteem while enhancing the quality of your relationships.

Lastly, the notion of 'what you can be paid for' may seem irrelevant in personal relationships, but when taken metaphorically, it opens new insights. What rewards do you receive in your relationships? Not material or financial, but emotional and spiritual. Perhaps through relationships, you're "paid" in happiness, understanding, mirrored growth, or shared experiences.

In the pursuit of enhancing personal relationships with Ikigai, remember to stay authentic. This isn't about changing yourself to fit into someone else's life or making sacrifices that leave you feeling unfulfilled. It's about aligning your interactions in a way that brings joy and fulfillment to you while also benefitting your loved ones. Maintaining balance is crucial. The focus need not be on perfect equilibrium. Instead, let your interactions flow naturally. You may realize that there are more aspects of 'what you love' with one person, 'what the world needs' in another relationship, and so forth. Such diversity in your relationships can offer a richer, more vibrant social landscape.

Embodying Ikigai in our relationships encourages us

to be intentional, mindful, and present. It helps us to appreciate the unique dynamics in every relationship and to foster connections that echo our own personal truths. So in your journey of Ikigai, let your relationships bloom as a gorgeous, vibrant field of interconnected Ikigai flowers, each bond distinct yet beautifully contributing to the astonishing wonder that is your life.

The Role of Community in Finding Your Ikigai

The journey to discover one's Ikigai is deeply personal, but it is certainly not solitary. The role of community is crucial to finding one's being and promoting a balanced and fulfilling existence. By community we mean the network of people around us: family, friends, colleagues, classmates, neighbors, mentors, even our broader digital community.

Many of us live our lives interconnected. In this interconnection, the community serves as a mirror, reflecting back parts of ourselves, helping identify our true convictions, values, strengths, passions, and even areas where the world needs us. They often see in us what we in our self-doubt or modesty may overlook.

For instance, you might not have considered your passion for gardening as more than an enjoyable pastime. However, your community could be the one to point out the positive impact you create through your hobby—say, by promoting sustainable living or spreading the joy of green spaces, thus indicating a possible alignment with 'what the world needs.'

Your professional community can also play a significant role in recognizing 'what you are good at.' Your value in the workplace or industry might seem ordinary to you. But coworkers and mentors can often pinpoint unique skills or strengths that distinctly set you apart. This valuable feedback can align with the 'what you can be paid for' aspect of Ikigai, broadening your perspective on your professional potential.

Your community can support your pursuit of Ikigai with emotional support, validation, encouragement, guidance, and practical help. This support can be a revitalizing source of external motivation, especially at times when internal motivation wavers.

Community engagement can also provide opportunities to put your personal research into practice, allowing you to explore, experiment, adjust and then refine your understanding of what gives your life meaning. Whether it is a local group that shares your hobby, a professional network aligned with your field of interest, a volunteer organization that engages in social causes important to you, or digital communities that connect individuals with similar aspirations, these platforms can significantly enrich your journey of personal discovery

A community filled with vibrant diversity offers a rich landscape of inspiration for finding your Ikigai. Observing others—how they navigate their passions, professions, vocations, services to the world—can provide valuable insights and trigger introspections, inspiriting you in your Ikigai voyage. As you tread this path, remember that vulnerability plays a vital role in connecting with your community. Be open about your journey, share your discoveries, express your uncertainties, and you'll find that this authenticity not only enriches your relationships but also fortifies your connection to your community, creating a strong support system in your Ikigai quest.

So your community can act as a robust lighthouse, guiding and illuminating your path as you navigate towards your Ikigai. Embrace their presence, learn, and grow through the interactions, and you would find your journey towards identifying and living your Ikigai becoming incredibly meaningful, insightful, and fulfilling.

Balancing Work, Life, and Passion

Embracing your Ikigai involves blending various aspects of your existence—your passions, the needs of the world, your skills, and what can sustain you financially. Finding the common ground among these facets encourages a balanced approach to career, leisure, and passion, nurturing a life that is both meaningful and satisfying.

Balancing work, life, and passion is an ongoing process, but let's discuss some strategies that could facilitate achieving this balance.

Aligning work with elements of your Ikigai can ensure your professional life contributes to your overall happiness, instead of standing as a separate, often stressful, domain. Here, work becomes a detailed choreography of your passion, mission, vocation, profession—making work feel less like a duty and more like a joyous expedition of personal realization.

Nurturing a hobby, passion, or personal interest forms a crucial aspect of this balancing act. Time spent away from work engaging in an activity you love can provide a wonderful counterbalance to your professional obligations. This 'me-time' can rejuvenate your spirit, fuel creativity, bolster energy levels and inject joy into your life.

Now, it's crucial to make sure that your relationships remain a priority, balanced alongside your career and personal interests. These relationships, whether familial, platonic, or romantic, add depth to our lives, provide emotional support and contribute to our overall sense of happiness and belonging. Scheduling quality time for loved ones, turning dedicating undistracted moments for connecting, mutually supporting each other's passions can ensure relationships thrive amidst the hustle of daily life.An often overlooked but essential element in this equation is self-care—physical, emotional, and mental. Regular physical activity, an effective stress management routine, and maintaining a nutritious diet becomes the bedrock supporting the balance. Remember, you cannot pour from an empty cup.

Getting organized stands as another ally in this pursuit. Efficient time management, prioritizing tasks, setting boundaries, and delegating duties when possible can ensure work and passions receive your attention without consuming every moment, leaving room for relaxation and relationships.

It's crucial to affirm that the objective is not perfection but validation of all aspects of your life—work, life, and passion. There will be days where work might claim more from us, other days where our passion or personal lives might demand attention. Even in this shift, remember, you're balancing on a seesaw and not walking on a tight rope. There will be ups and downs, forward and backward sways, but the essence lies in continuously striving for equilibrium.

Embrace this journey of balancing work, life, and passion, as it fosters personal growth, challenges you to improve, and encourages a holistic blend of all life aspects. And most importantly, it propels you alongside your path of Ikigai, ensuring you're not just surviving your days, but truly living them.

Activities to Enrich Your Daily Routine

Integrating Ikigai into your daily routine not only inspires a sense of purpose but also enriches your day, filling you with joy, fulfillment, and a sense of achievement.
Here are a few practices to weave into your daily routine that align with the various aspects of Ikigai.

Initiate your day with an activity you love—it could be reading a chapter of a book, indulging in an early yoga session, working on a craft project, or even listening to an inspiring podcast. Introducing elements of your passion to your morning routine sets a positive tone for the day.

Next, find time during the day for skill-building. If your Ikigai involves a skill you aren't yet proficient at, dedicate a part of your day to hone it. This could involve online courses, reading relevant books, or practicing the skill. Not only are you 'doing what you're good at,' but you're fostering continuous improvement vital on the path of Ikigai.
In the realm of 'what the world needs,' consider volunteering or contributing your skills to a community or niche group. Joining local community clubs, supporting a cause or an NGO, or mentoring

someone in your field of expertise can be deeply rewarding.

Towards the end of your day, take some time for introspection. Reflect upon your daily activities—your feelings, interactions, accomplishments, even shortcomings. Journaling is a brilliant way to practice this self-reflection, enabling you to acknowledge your progress on the Ikigai journey and gain insightful perspectives for future actions.
Finally, ensure you have sufficient downtime. Seek balance by resting, relaxing and rejuvenating. Whether it's cooking a meal, soaking in a warm bath, catching a TV show, immersing in a relaxing hobby or simply doing nothing—remember, self-care is a valid, integral part of finding and living your Ikigai.

By integrating these activities, your daily routine is transformed into a vibrant mosaic of joyful engagement, personal growth, meaningful connections and intentional action, all reflecting a life rich in purpose. A daily routine enriched in this way promotes a sense of fulfillment, harmonizes your daily life with your deepest goals, and fosters the development of a balanced, fulfilling existence in harmony with self. Remember that each day represents an opportunity, a blank canvas ready to be painted with the unique colors of your passion and purpose..

Sustaining Your Ikigai

The Challenges of Maintaining Ikigai

Discovering one's Ikigai is like embarking on an exciting and transformative expedition, but once found, maintaining it can present a number of obstacles. It is important to recognize these challenges, as they paint a realistic picture of the Ikigai journey and prepare one to face these obstacles with an informed and resilient mindset.

The very first challenge often lies in maintaining a balance between the four elements of Ikigai—what you love, what the world needs, what you're good at, and what you can be paid for. Overemphasis on one element or negligence of another can create disruptions in the delicate harmony of Ikigai. Balancing professional obligations, personal interests, relationships, societal contributions can be akin to juggling on a tightrope. However, embracing flexibility, practicing patience, and thorough self-awareness can equip us to navigate this balancing act adeptly.

Second, as human beings, we are constantly evolving; our interests, passions and abilities are constantly changing and growing. This fluid nature can lead to a change in our goals and aspirations over time, posing a challenge. Adapting to these changes while remaining true to one's goals may seem like a daunting challenge. However, remember that the pursuit of purpose in life is not an immutable concept. A goal that changes over time simply reflects your personal growth and requires continual reevaluation and realignment with your core values and aspirations.

Procrastination can appear as a daunting challenge, too. There might be tasks associated with your Ikigai that, for various reasons, you tend to procrastinate. Fearing judgment, lacking self-confidence, or simply the perceived enormity of a task can lead to putting it off. Overcoming procrastination requires cultivating discipline, breaking tasks into manageable parts, and consciously working towards creating workflows that align with your Ikigai.

Societal pressures and expectations can often cloud our search for purpose. Social conventions regarding career choices, financial success, or lifestyles can make it difficult to identify our true purpose. In such cases, in order to keep our internal compass oriented toward what really matters to us, it is essential to ground ourselves, reconnect with our deepest beliefs, and prioritize our own personal evaluation over the pursuit of social approval.

The quest to maintain Ikigai could, at times, feel isolating. There may be instances of self-doubt, moments when you question the whole endeavor. In such times, the wisdom lies in reaching out, connecting with others on similar journeys, indulging in open conversations, and seeking support from your community.

Recognizing these challenges on the path to achieving your goals does not diminish their importance, but rather strengthens your resolve, promotes resilience and pragmatic optimism in your personal journey. As you brace yourself to face these challenges, remember that each hurdle is a stepping stone, each obstacle a new lesson, and every challenge an opportunity for growth. With the wisdom to appreciate these challenges and the courage to confront them, you'll find your bond with your Ikigai not only enduring but thriving and blossoming into a more authentic, stronger alignment with your true self.

Long-term Strategies
for Ikigai Preservation

After examining the challenges of maintaining Ikigai, the next step is to equip ourselves with long-term strategies for preservation over time. Armed with these strategies, we can effectively navigate the rough sea of challenges and keep ourselves anchored in our Ikigai.

One principal strategy is regular self-reflection. An ongoing dialogue with self helps keep a check on our progress, keep our motivations fresh and facilitates realignments if necessary. This could involve journaling, meditation, or even a quiet few minutes each day dedicated to introspection.

Another vital strategy is to create and maintain a supportive community. This community can consist of mentors, loved ones, or even online forums. They can provide valuable feedback, offer alternate perspectives, appreciate your growth, and provide emotional support during challenging times. Consistent skill improvement forms another cornerstone for preserving your Ikigai. The world is continually evolving, and so must our abilities to stay relevant and accomplish 'what one can be paid for.' Regular training, classes, reading, or any activity enhancing your skills can feed into this long-term strategy.

Setting small, achievable goals connected to your Ikigai can provide a sense of direction and encouragement in your journey. These goals need not be colossal; they could be as simple as dedicating a few hours each week to a hobby you love or completing a short course to enhance your skills.

Learning to manage stress and prioritizing self-care should be an integral part of any long-term Ikigai preservation strategy. Balancing work, life, and passion can sometimes become overwhelming. Periodic relaxation, hobbies that make you happy, physical activities, and mindfulness techniques can contribute to efficient stress management.

Embracing flexibility and adaptability stands as yet another potent strategy. Opportunities might arise where you can expand or alter your roles in both personal and professional life to more closely align with your essence. Be open to these changes and be willing to experiment.

Cultivate resilience. Each challenge faced in the Ikigai preservation journey is an opportunity for growth, learning, and to become stronger. Adopting a resilient mindset encourages a positive outlook and provides the courage to tackle challenges head-on.
A point to remember throughout this journey is that preserving Ikigai is not about creating a set plan and rigidly sticking to it. Rather, it's about having a direction, being aware of possible deterrents, equipping ourselves with effective strategies, and navigating our way, one day at a time, in the vast seas of life towards our Ikigai.

Ikigai and Mental Health

The connection between Ikigai and mental health is profound, creating a ripple effect that transcends beyond personal fulfillment to influencing overall psychological well-being. The intertwining of mental health and Ikigai is a topic that deserves exploration as it illuminates how deeply our innermost purpose and passion can impact our emotional and cognitive health. At its core, Ikigai revolves around purpose. Numerous research has shown that having a purpose in life, a direction, a deep sense of why we do what we do, significantly bolsters our mental health. It actively contributes to happiness, reduces chances of depression, enhances resilience, and even promotes longevity.

Living our Ikigai provides a bountiful source of intrinsic motivation— motivation that springs from within and stands independent of external rewards. This stabilizes our drive to carry on, regroup after failures, and combat procrastination, thereby directly contributing to enhanced mood, greater self-esteem, and sturdier mental health.

Ikigai, with its core principle of discovering and nurturing what we love, infuses joy in our lives. This element of joy acts as a strong ally in combating mental health issues like stress, anxiety, and sadness. By striving for what we love, we are continuously creating happiness, contributing to our positive mental health bank.

A fundamental aspect of the personal quest for purpose is service: understanding the needs of the world and contributing through our unique abilities and passions. Acts of service have been associated with increased happiness, a deep sense of satisfaction and enhanced emotional well-being.

Living a life aligned with our personal purpose encourages us to harness and develop our strengths. This continual usage and recognition of our abilities foster a positive self-image, enhances self-esteem, and enables us to appreciate our uniqueness and worth more authentically, fortifying our psychological health.

At the same time, it is imperative to keep in mind that the journey to and with the search for one's purpose can itself be challenging and fulfilling. Embracing this quest does not mean an end to mental health struggles. However, during times of fluctuating mental health, remembering our purpose can give us motivation and direction, serving as an emotional anchor in the tumultuous sea of psychological distress.

In addition, practicing the search for one's purpose helps develop what experts call 'psychological flexibility.' It encourages us to accept our feelings, adapt to changes and voluntarily change our course of action, promoting healthier emotional regulation strategies.

Ikigai research and practice can powerfully supplement our mental health toolkit. Its intrinsically motivational, passion-driven, service-based, and forceful approach makes Ikigai not only a mechanism for personal development, but also a vital companion on our journey to mental health. Therefore, as we continue to cultivate our vital essence, we also celebrate the beautiful positive impact it has on our mental health, further emphasizing that cultivating our Ikigai actually means preserving our holistic well-being.

The Future of Ikigai in Your Life

A journey with Ikigai isn't solely about the present—about now, today, this moment. It's a lifelong path that extends into the future, shaping the course of our individual growth and personal self-realization. As you further incorporate and practice the principles of

Ikigai in your life, let's consider what the future may hold for you.

The most profound effect you'd witness in the future is an enhanced sense of alignment and harmony between your inner self and outer life. Living your Ikigai blurs the lines between work and play, between duty and joy. Conventional constructs of 'work-life balance' give way to a 'work-life mix' that makes each day more rewarding and fulfilling. Your career path may be transformed, realigning more with what you find truly meaningful and exciting in life. You could find yourself pursuing a career path more resonant with your passions and values, proving both rewarding and enjoyable. If shifts in career aren't possible or desirable, you may find ways to introduce aspects of your Ikigai into your current profession, making it an integral part of your journey.

Your relationships could flourish too. By living your Ikigai, you live authentically, and authentic lives foster genuine relationships. You become more attuned to your needs and those of others, enhancing empathy and understanding in your relationships.
Personal development stands as another illuminating facet in your future Ikigai journey. As you continue your exploration, refining skills, adapting to changes, overcoming challenges, you'll experience comprehensive growth, mentally, emotionally and spiritually. This process, over time, crafts a better, resilient, adaptable, and more self-aware version of yourself.

Your influence in the world can expand in unbelievable ways. As you align more with 'what the world needs,' your contribution to society becomes more substantial and impactful. You may find yourself participating more in community-building, extending your skills for public good, fostering beneficial changes in your environment—big or small.

Exploring and living according to one's purpose also has the potential to enrich one's mental health over time. A greater sense of purpose, happiness and personal fulfillment can strengthen resilience, emotional strength and overall mental well-being.
Over the course of a lifetime, you may notice changes in your purpose. With personal growth, life experiences and changes in perspective, what motivates and inspires you may evolve. These changes are natural and healthy, marking the evolution of your being.

Your future with Ikigai is a prospect filled with potential, growth, evolution, and deepening alignment with your authentic self. It's a journey that promises enrichment of your life on multiple fronts—personal, professional, societal, intellectual, and emotional. As you step into this exciting, transforming future, remember to embrace each phase with acceptance, courage, and unyielding curiosity. Explore, evolve, grow—And know that through all the undulations of life, your Ikigai serves as your compass, guiding you towards your authentic self, a fulfilling life, and your unique mark in the world. Your Ikigai journey, hence, crafts not just an enriching path for now, but also a promising, luminous map for your future.

Continuing Your Ikigai Journey

The journey towards discovering and living your Ikigai isn't a destination to reach, but a path to tread on progressively, every single day. The path may sometimes be challenging, the future may sometimes seem uncertain, and the steps may sometimes feel heavy, but remember, each step you take is a step forward. The beauty of this personal journey lies not in the final destination, but in the path itself, in the continuous exploration and growth it promises. Let's examine how you can continue this journey, making it a fundamental part of your life.

Firstly, keep nurturing your self-awareness. Continue the practice of introspection and self-reflection. Keep asking yourself the Ikigai questions and listen to the responses your heart and soul present. Your Ikigai might shift with time, evolve with experiences, and thus it is vital to maintain this ongoing dialogue with your inner self. Continue your pursuit of learning and development. Irrespective of where you stand in your life, there's always something new to learn, an aspect to improve, a skill to refine. Maintain this growth mindset, for it's instrumental in both discovering and living your Ikigai.

Maintain connections with your community as you continue this journey. Not only can they provide valuable perspectives and feedback, but they also serve as a source of motivation and inspiration. Lean into these connections, and you'll find your path illuminated by their shared wisdom and experiences.

Practice resilience. Not every day on this journey is going to be easy. There will be days of doubt, days of confusion, days of setback. However, on those days, remind yourself of the progress you've made, remember your Ikigai, and know that every challenge is an opportunity for growth.

Celebrate the small victories. Every small step you take in the direction of your goals, every small change you make, every small action, should be celebrated. These small victories add up over time, leading to significant transformation and progress. Above all, be patient with yourself. The journey to personal fulfillment is not a race, but a lifelong quest. Do not put pressure on yourself to find all the answers immediately or to achieve drastic changes instantly. Allow yourself the time and space to explore, learn and evolve.

Finally, as you continue your Ikigai journey, remember to enjoy the process. Embrace the journey with its ups and downs, its joys and challenges. Find joy in exploration, pride in growth and joy in the gradual alignment of your daily life with your Ikigai. This journey after all is filled with deep personal insights, invigorating growth and graceful alignment of your actions with your deepest truths.

Continue on your path, stride forward with determination and drive, interspersed with moments of quiet reflection and celebration. You have embarked on one of the most rewarding journeys of your life. It's a path leading you to a life rich in fulfillment and authenticity. Harness the power of Ikigai in every step, and you'll find your days brimming with purpose, passion, and a profound sense of living true to your unique self. Here's to your Ikigai journey, to a life lived with purpose, and to a personally resonant legacy you're creating each day!

.Kaizen

改善

The Art of Continuous Improvement:
The Principles of Kaizen

Introduction to Kaizen and Its Origins

At its heart, Kaizen is a mindset. A philosophy rooted in Japan, it comprises of two words 'Kai', meaning change, and 'Zen', meaning goodness or betterness. Together, Kaizen translates to 'change for the better'

or 'continuous improvement.' Its origins are deeply interwoven in the Japanese culture and work ethos, where the spirit of diligence, commitment to efficient work, and the quest for continuous betterment are all held in high regard.

However, the application of Kaizen as a formal process improvement methodology sprouted in the post-World War II Japanese manufacturing sector. Much of its development is credited to the "father of quality control," W. Edwards Deming. Deming, an American statistician, was invited by Japanese industrial leaders to help revive their economy. He propounded the idea of quality control circles—a platform where workers gather to discuss work-related problems and brainstorm solutions for quality improvement. This egalitarian model created a conducive environment for the essence of Kaizen to flourish.

Over time, the principle of continuous improvement has transcended the boundaries of factories, finding application in a wide range of sectors: from business management to health care, from education to personal development. Its effectiveness and applicability have made it an essential component of Lean Manufacturing methodologies, a pillar of Six Sigma principles, and a key element of Total Quality Management. In the context of personal development, this principle introduces the illuminating idea that significant change is the result of many small steps taken over time. It places emphasis on the importance of gradual progress, encouraging people to pursue personal improvement steadily, without being overwhelmed by the ambition to achieve grandiose goals at once.

The journey of Kaizen, beginning as an industrial

philosophy to becoming an influential global phenomenon, holds a profound lesson for our personal lives. It validates the power of consistent, small steps in crafting significant transformations. It whispers an empowering possibility—you don't have to undertake monumental changes to transform yourself; start small, be steady, and watch as the ripples of these small changes expand into a wave of personal transformation.

As we begin to delve deeper into the principles of Kaizen and elucidate its profound implications in personal and professional life, let's take this understanding with us: every small step, every subtle change, every act of patience and persistence, is powerful. They are the building blocks for growth, the steps to sustainable success and the essence of Kaizen— the change, that in its smallness, contains the potential for true and lasting betterment.

The 5 Core Elements of Kaizen

An exploration into the principles of Kaizen leads us to its five key elements. These principles are at the heart of continuous improvement, guiding us on a journey of constant growth, success and progress.

The first fundamental pillar of this approach is self-discipline. Without it, the engine of progress is in danger of stalling. Integrating self-discipline into our daily lives enables us to define and follow productive routines, achieve set goals, and maintain high standards of quality in both our work and personal lives.

The second element is teamwork. Kaizen encourages active involvement of everyone in the process of improvement. This principle emphasizes that every voice matters, every opinion counts. By fostering a culture of teamwork, Kaizen makes space for diverse ideas, perspectives, and solutions, collectively contributing to significant improvements.

Quality consciousness forms the third element. It encourages individuals and teams to strive for superior quality in all aspects of work and life. By cultivating quality consciousness, one is encouraged to uphold high standards, reduce errors, and ensure that the outcome of any task, big or small, is the best it can be.

The fourth element revolves around suggestive improvements. Kaizen firmly believes in the power of small steps leading to big changes. Every suggestion, however minute, when implemented, contributes to the overall improvement. Encouraging suggestive improvements opens avenues for continuous betterment and nurtures a culture of innovation and creativity.

The fifth and final element is the ongoing process of improvement. Kaizen is not a destination but a journey, where the process of continuous improvement never ends. Once a change has been implemented and the results have been observed, there's always room for further fine-tuning, optimization, and again, improvement.

If these five basic principles of continuous improvement are applied with dedication and a progress-oriented spirit, they can trigger significant transformations. From increasing productivity and performance to improving the quality of work and promoting personal satisfaction, collaboration and innovation, the guidelines offered by this approach are a valuable resource for progress at both the individual and organizational levels.

As you begin to incorporate the principles of Kaizen into your life journey, remember to celebrate each small improvement, imbuing them with the appreciation and importance they deserve. These individual steps, each powered by self-discipline, teamwork, quality consciousness, suggestive improvements, and an indefatigable spirit of ongoing progress, are the steps to transformation and success in the journey of life. In the delicate interplay of these elements, the philosophy of Kaizen truly comes alive, empowering each of us to become better versions of ourselves, one small step at a time.

Kaizen in Personal Development

The philosophy of Kaizen, while initially conceptualized for industrial processes, lends itself beautifully to the realm of personal development. The concept of continual, incremental improvements converges seamlessly with personal growth, enriching and iterating upon how we perceive and employ self-improvement concepts. In our lives, large goals can often seem daunting—learning a new language, picking up a new skill, losing weight, or even finding our 'Ikigai.' The fear of the overwhelming effort required can sometimes inhibit us from even commencing our journey. This is where Kaizen steps in, gently reminding us that substantial changes materialize from consistent, small steps.

Let's consider an individual aiming to develop a

reading habit but is put off by the mammoth-sized books or the enormous time commitment. Employing Kaizen, they begin by reading just a page or two daily. This mini goal is manageable, non-intimidating, setting the stage for the habit forming process. Over time, they gradually increase the reading span. This small, incremental progress eventually culminates in the development of a strong, consistent reading habit and a newfound love for books.

Even in personal relationships, applying small, constant adjustments can have a profound impact. If the goal is to improve communication with one's partner, trying to completely revamp it overnight may be overwhelming and met with resistance. By opting for the gradual introduction of minor changes, such as devoting an extra five minutes each day to distraction-free conversation, listening carefully and valuing the other person's point of view, these small steps can accumulate, leading to more effective dialogue and a stronger relationship.

Self-improvement is integral to personal development. While the desire to become 'an overnight sensation' might seem tempting, the Kaizen way encourages us to be patient with ourselves, to acknowledge that worthwhile development happens over time. A minute of meditation can lead to peaceful hours. A small step to organize your work could lead to days of productivity. A small course could open doors to new career opportunities.

By focusing on the process and taking baby steps towards our goals, we can alleviate the pressure, making the journey of personal development more enjoyable and sustainable. Through its teachings, Kaizen revolutionizes our approach to personal development, reinforcing the belief that every step forward, no matter how small, is a positive stride towards growth.

So let the small-step approach guide your path to personal growth. Approach your most ambitious goals with kindness and patience, recognizing the value of incrementality, and you will soon see how significant changes originate from modest beginnings. In approaching this path, keep in mind that the true essence of this approach lies not just in achieving a specific goal, but in adopting a steady, gradual process of development, one small step after another.

Kaizen in the Workplace: Case Studies

If we turn our gaze to the professional sphere, we find that the concept of Kaizen is bearing rich fruit, increasing efficiency and promoting a culture of continuous improvement. Numerous organizations globally have ingrained these principles in their ethics and reaped significant benefits. We explore some case studies to illustrate personal growth in action in the workplace.

A striking example comes to us from the world-admired automaker Toyota. The integration of progressive improvement principles in Toyota led to the birth of the renowned Toyota Production System. At the heart of this system is the elimination of waste and continuous improvement, key elements of its ethos. Employees were empowered to stop the assembly line upon the detection of any mishap, thus highlighting a deep commitment to quality. This methodology helped decrease waste, increase productivity and improve product quality, strengthening Toyota's reputation as an industry pioneer.

In healthcare, Virginia Mason Medical Center stands out as an organization that adopted Kaizen and transformed its patient-care and administration. Delays, high costs, and other inefficiencies haunted the hospital. They opted to develop a culture focused on constant evolution by embracing the philosophy of small progressive steps. Among the actions taken were standardization of equipment and procedures, active involvement of all staff in problem-solving projects, and restructuring of care processes. These changes have led to a marked improvement in patient outcomes, considerable cost savings, and increased satisfaction among staff members.

AT&T, the telecom giant, implemented Kaizen workshops to tackle their issue of long service delivery times. The process involved every stakeholder, identifying bottlenecks, emphasizing preventing errors, focusing on continuous improvement. The result? Significant improvement of service delivery time, from 13.9 to 8 days on average and better workforce collaboration.

Another case study zooms in on Lockheed Martin, renowned aerospace manufacturer, that deployed Kaizen to enhance their productivity, implementing projects across production lines, waste reduction, and continuous improvement became an organizational intent. The outcomes were impressive—increased productivity, reduced wastage, significant cost savings, and a more motivated workforce.

Each of these organizations, despite their diverse industries, found the essence and application of Kaizen to be a valuable asset. The strength of continuous improvement in work settings lies in its ability to involve all members of the organization: no idea is too modest, no contribution is insignificant. This generates a unique sense of community, stimulating motivation and job satisfaction.

These practical examples offer valuable lessons. The application of principles of constant evolution, regardless of scope, can result in significant effects: from increased productivity to decreased costs, from refinement of product or service quality to staff involvement and contentment. It clearly demonstrates how every small step toward refinement is relevant and contributes to substantial company-wide transformations.

In your career, whether you are in leadership positions or are a member of a team, adopting the principles of incremental progress can reveal a universe of relentless development, dedication to quality, and creating an environment that values the contribution of each person.

Consider Kaizen not just as a tool for business management, but as a philosophy fostering growth, efficiency, and a satisfying work environment.

Daily Practices for Kaizen

Taking the leap from understanding Kaizen to implementing its principles in daily life can appear daunting. To ease this transition, here are some concrete strategies for integrating the principle of step-by-step improvement into your daily routine.

Begin by setting a mini goal but link it with a broader purpose or goal. If learning to play piano forms your larger goal, start with something manageable, like practicing scales for 15 minutes each day.

This small step is your Kaizen action, feeding into your bigger purpose of mastering the piano. Try to develop a daily routine. As mundane as it may sound, a routine provides a structure, paving the road for consistency. Creating a well-organized routine that includes small daily milestones helps to progressively develop habits that support the achievement of more meaningful goals, thus reflecting the step-by-step approach to improvement. Use the principle of suggestive improvements. Each day, question how you can improve your major life areas—health, work, relationships, or personal growth. Don't strive for major improvements, but seek out small, manageable changes that can contribute to significant benefits over time.

Practice mindfulness to foster quality consciousness. Be attentive to your daily tasks, small or big. On its surface, this practice promotes higher performance and efficiency, but on a deeper level, it nurtures an appreciation for the process—crucial for the Kaizen journey.

Lastly, review your progress periodically. Reflect on your journey every week, acknowledging the small improvements, the baby steps you've taken towards your larger goal. These moments of reflection serve as motivational fuel, encouraging further progress.

Fundamentally, Kaizen isn't about attaining perfection; rather, it's about making consistent efforts towards improvement, transformation, and growth. Remember, the destination isn't as important as the journey. Enjoy the process, the small victories, the daily improvements.

Setting and Achieving Goals with Kaizen

Breaking Down Large Goals

The approach to goal setting with a step-by-step improvement mindset differs markedly from the tendency to set broad goals that can be intimidating. This philosophy encourages dividing goals into smaller, more manageable components, extolling the value of smaller but steady progress that, when added together, leads to significant change.

Take, for example, the ambition to complete a marathon. Taken as a whole, this goal may appear imposing. However, by adopting a step-by-step approach, the goal becomes more accessible: we start by setting small intermediate steps, making the final goal easier to conquer. The first step might be to run for just five minutes a day. That's it. A simple, non-intimidating, easily achievable task that gets you moving. Over time, consistently adding an extra minute or two to your run eventually leads you to the point where running a marathon does not seem like an insurmountable task, but a reasonable progression of your consistent efforts.

This principle can be applied to any large goal. Wish to write a book? Start by committing to write a page each day. Want to become fluent in a new language? Learn a few phrases every day. The trick here is not to get fixated on the enormity of the final goal but focus on the action you can take right now, however small it might be.

The magic of Kaizen lies in these smaller blocks of success. They are approachable, reducing the fear or resistance that larger goals often arouse. These diminutive steps, by their nature, increase the likelihood of consistency, setting the stage for a habit, and reducing the need for extreme willpower or motivation. Breaking down large goals into smaller steps also brings the goal closer to reality, from the abstract to the concrete. It provides a clear, actionable roadmap, nudging you to progress from inertia to motion, setting the wheel of progress in continuous rotation.

Remember, your journey towards achieving your goals is not a sprint, but a marathon. Running full speed might bring immediate gains, but it's the steady, consistent pace that ensures you reach the finish line. This is what Kaizen promotes—steady, small steps accumulating into a sweeping wave of change and achievement.

Therefore, regardless of whether your focus is on personal development or achieving professional goals, fragment your big goals into smaller, manageable activities. Use the cumulative effect of these small steps to move closer to your ambitious goal, adopting the spirit of gradual progress as your guide on your path to achievement and success. every journey of a thousand miles begins with a single step. Make that step measured, steady and in perfect accordance with the principles of continuous improvement.

The Role of Habit
Formation in Kaizen

At the heart of Kaizen lies the power of habit. Habits are what shape our lives, dictate our actions, and ultimately determine our success or failure. Thus, the true effectiveness of progressive improvement lies not only in introducing an isolated change, but in creating a dynamic of constant evolution and improvement.

But why do habits play such a crucial role in this process? Mainly, because they make progress more accessible. Do you wish to read fifty books in a year? This goal may seem impressive. However, establishing the habit of reading a few pages every day makes the goal less intimidating and more manageable.

Secondly, habits, once formed, require minimal conscious effort or motivation to maintain. When actions transform into habits, they become automatic, eliminating the consistent need for willpower and reducing the likelihood of resistance and procrastination.

Furthermore, habits reinforce progress. Even small habitual actions, when taken consistently, lead to substantial gains over time and make a significant impact on goal achievement. Let's consider a person wanting to improve their well-being. Instead of embracing a stringent diet or a strenuous workout regime, they begin by incorporating a simple workout routine—10 minutes of walking daily. It's a dollop-sized task, easy to stick to, and unlikely to trigger resistance. Over time, this small habit of walking for 10 minutes can be built upon—increasing the duration, perhaps adding yoga, leading to substantial improvements in fitness and well-being.

Building habits is also a lesson in patience and self-compassion. The fruit of habits—the substantial changes—are not immediately evident. They appear gradually, silently. So, sticking to the course, even when results appear slow, is crucial. Understanding that setbacks don't signal failure but are part of the process also plays a key in successfully implementing and maintaining habits.

Molding practices according to Kaizen principles and habit formation theory can, therefore, have profound effects. Embedding small positive habits in your daily routine can edify your personal growth, improve your professional skills, enhance your health, and aid in fostering better relationships.
They are the threads that weave our daily life. Through the lens of Kaizen, habit formation becomes

a means of transforming these threads into a strong, sustainable path towards continuous improvement. Embrace the power of habits, taking small steps consistently, handle the ebbs and flows with patience and resilience, and watch as you steadily travel towards your desired goals.

As Aristotle stated beautifully, "We are what we repeatedly do. Excellence, then, is not an act, but a habit." Let's strive to craft habits of excellence, one tiny step at a time, echoing the spirit of Kaizen in our everyday lives.

Measuring Progress and Setting Milestones

In the Kaizen journey, taking consistent steps towards betterment forms a significant part of the process, but an equally pivotal aspect is tracking that progress. Monitoring and evaluating progress serves two purposes. It provides valuable feedback on the effectiveness of your actions and serves as a motivator, reflecting the tangible results of your small, consistent efforts.

Effectively measuring progress and setting milestones are crucial steps in the context of continuous improvement, essential for staying the course and recognizing achievements along the way. The very ethos of Kaizen—making small incremental changes—allows for an easily trackable progression. As you embark on your goal-achievement path, create a daily log or journal to document these changes.

Suppose you've started practicing yoga for fifteen

minutes daily. Every day, make a note of your experience, the change in your flexibility, the impact on your stress levels or overall mood. Over time, you will have a record that explicitly portrays your progress and the cumulative impact of those fifteen-minute sessions.

It's vital to remember that progress isn't always linear, and setbacks or plateaus are part of the journey. Using a progress log will help you understand, analyze, and adjust your actions based on these occasional dips. If a particular step doesn't seem to be yielding the expected results, instead of getting discouraged, use this opportunity to revise your strategy. Setting milestones is another invaluable tool in your Kaizen journey. An integral part of goal-setting, milestones act as markers on your path, providing you an occasion to pause, review and celebrate your progress.
Imagine you're working on a project that will take several months, if not years, to complete. Large projects can often seem overwhelming, but setting milestones can make the project more manageable. Allocate specific checkpoints where you can measure your progress. Each time you hit a milestone, it validates the effectiveness of your Kaizen actions.

Ensure that they're designed not to intimidate but to inspire and motivate. Perhaps completing a chapter of the book you're writing, or achieving a specific weight loss target, or successfully delivering a public speech.

Measurement of progress and setting milestones in your journey bestows value beyond just assessing the effectiveness of your actions. They serve as a torchbearer, illuminating your path, giving you a fair account of where you stand and how much you have traversed. They provide a sense of accomplishment and validation, solidifying your confidence, and adding more fuel to your motivation.

As you proceed on this journey, remember that Kaizen is a transformative process. Take small actions, keep a record of each step, and celebrate each milestone. Amid setbacks, find guidance in your records, refine your steps, and stay steadfast on your path. Progress, as they say, is more about the journey than the destination. So, relish each step, savor each milestone, and embrace the journey towards continuous improvement through the power of Kaizen.

Stories of Personal Achievement

The elegance of the Kaizen philosophy emerges when its principles are applied in real-life situations, leading to personal achievements.
Let's look at some examples of individuals who have adopted the step-by-step progress approach to make significant changes and achieve their goals. Consider the story of Amelia, who, after years of battling obesity, made her health her priority. Instead of taking up an extreme diet or fitness regime, she adopted Kaizen. Amelia began by committing to just 10 minutes of walking daily. As this practice slowly became a habit over weeks, she added a few more minutes to her walks, eventually incorporating light workouts. Two years later, Amelia had lost over 50 pounds, significantly improved her health, and developed a sustainable exercise habit.

Or let's take Alvin's story. As a writer grappling with

writer's block, he found writing anything longer than a few sentences overwhelming. When he discovered the Kaizen method, he decided to apply its principles. He committed to writing just one sentence per day. This tiny goal removed the pressure previously associated with his writing. Gradually, one sentence evolved into two, two into a paragraph, until gradually an entire chapter was completed.

Then there's Farah, who always coveted better organization at work but failed to stick to productivity systems because they felt too rigid and overwhelming. She decided to try the Kaizen approach. Farah chose to start by organizing just one aspect of her work: her email inbox. She began by dedicating five minutes each day to maintaining her inbox. The change was small enough to feel manageable, and soon she started using those five minutes productively. As she saw the benefits, she decided to slowly incorporate other small organizational habits creating a system that was gradual, comfortable and eventually led to significant improvements in her productivity.

Each of these stories showcases the transformative power of Kaizen. Goals that once seemed insurmountable were accomplished by taking small, manageable steps. The individuals eased into their transformations, and new habits were gradually ingrained. Their achievements were not overnight miracles but the result of consistent, persistent, incremental improvements—manifestations of Kaizen philosophy.

These stories of personal achievement are reminders that big changes can be born out of small consistent actions over time. Remember, there is power in starting small and never underestimating the potential of continuous, incremental improvement.

Listening to these stories, let's recognize and appreciate that our path to personal and professional achievement lies not in giant leaps, but in a series of small, consistent steps, leading us towards our goals, a step at a time. And that's the heart of Kaizen - a steady journey of personal transformation, one little step at a time.

Kaizen Goal-setting Workshop

A workshop focused on incremental progress for goal setting can be a game changer, allowing you to directly apply the principles of constant evolution to your life. In this section, we will explore how you can organize your own workshop based on this approach.

Start by listing your long-term goals or challenges that you'd like to tackle. Remember, the purpose of Kaizen is to turn these daunting tasks into achievable goals. Once you have the goals, scrutinize each task, breaking it down into its smallest components. This step aids in transforming the abstract into something concrete and manageable. For instance, if your goal is to read more books, instead of setting a vague goal like "read 30 books a year," break it down to "read 10 pages a day."

Now, you're ready to prioritize. Decide which goal you want to start working on first. Balance is key here. If one goal is particularly challenging, pair it with a simpler task. If your first goal is to run a marathon, perhaps your second goal could be something simpler, like waking up half an hour earlier. The blend of complex and simpler goals ensures you aren't overwhelmed and gives you quick wins to keep you motivated.

The next step is to establish a routine for these mini goals. Try to integrate them into your existing routine. This reduces the friction against the new habit. In our reading example, you could commit to reading your ten pages after breakfast each morning.

Set milestones. These intermediate targets give you a moment to reflect on your progress, adjust your course, if required, and celebrate your progress. For instance, reward yourself every time you finish a book.

Finally, the most crucial part—getting started. Ensuring a prompt start is quite possibly the most vital step. Don't wait for the perfect day or the perfect mood. The same evening you conduct your workshop, take the first step, no matter how small. If your goal is to read more, start by reading just one page.

Kaizen workshops are a practical way to apply the philosophy in your life. They allow you to turn intimidating tasks into manageable mini-goals, infuse them into your daily routine, and track your progress by setting milestones. Regularly revisiting and updating your workshop can make the journey of achieving your goals an enjoyable and satisfying process—a process where resistance gives way to progress, setting the stage for a lifelong journey of personal development and formidable successes. So, embrace the spirit of Kaizen in your goal-setting and make your way to constant improvement and lasting change.

Kaizen for Productivity and Efficiency

Tools and Techniques for Increasing Productivity

One of the merits of embracing the Kaizen approach lies in its tangible impact on productivity. Because the incremental progress-centered approach promotes constant self-improvement, it naturally provides you with tools and methods to increase productivity in various aspects of life. Let's look together at some of these valuable tools and techniques.

Consider the "Pomodoro Technique," a time management tool that breaks work into intervals, traditionally 25 minutes in length, separated by short breaks. This process aids in maintaining concentration and staving off mental fatigue, leading to enhanced productivity. Such a tool aligns beautifully with the philosophy of Kaizen, advocating consistent small steps to improve efficiency.

Then there's the "2-Minute Rule," a productivity strategy that suggests, "If it takes less than two minutes, then do it now." This simple rule helps to overcome procrastination, a common roadblock to productivity. Thus, the 2-Minute Rule encapsulates Kaizen's simple, actionable approach to fostering productivity.

Another useful tool is the "Eisenhower Box." It helps you prioritize your tasks by dividing them into four categories: Urgent and important (tasks you will do immediately), Important, but not urgent (tasks you will schedule to do later), Urgent, but not important (tasks you will delegate to someone else), and Neither urgent nor important (tasks that you will eliminate). This process of prioritization reduces clutter and enhances focus, ultimately leading to increased productivity, precisely mirroring Kaizen's emphasis on eliminating waste and streamlined actions.

One tool that deeply embodies the stepwise progress approach is constant self-reflection. Regularly evaluating your actions, acknowledging the successes, learning from failures, and adjusting your strategy is a powerful method to advance on the path of productivity. Data tracking and journaling can be instrumental tools in self-reflection.

Finally, realizing the power of habits is pivotal. We've discussed how breaking down goals into smaller tasks can make the journey towards achievement less daunting and more efficient. Similarly, transforming these small tasks into daily habits makes the process even smoother, effectively enhancing our productivity. Making a habit out of processes that contribute to your overall goals is a powerful way to harness Kaizen for your benefit.

The above-mentioned techniques and tools aren't novel or groundbreaking – in fact, they are quite simple. And therein lies their strength. They represent the essence of the progressive improvement approach, demonstrating that even minor changes, if implemented regularly, can culminate in major changes. By embracing these productivity-enhancing tools and techniques, you're not just streamlining your processes but aligning your work and personal life with the enduring philosophy of Kaizen. You embark on a journey where every step, no matter how small, takes you closer to your goals, fosters your personal and professional growth, and contributes to a life brimming with achievement and satisfaction. Remember, within the arena of productivity and efficiency, slow and steady does win the race.

Eliminating Waste in Your Daily Life and Work

Kaizen stands for continuous improvement, and an integral part of this journey involves the identification and elimination of waste. In a work context, 'waste' often translates to inefficiencies—actions that consume resources but don't add value.

Recognizing and eliminating waste benefits various aspects of your life. In your professional life, it could mean streamlined operations and enhanced productivity. In your personal life, it might signify more time for pursuits that truly matter.

The first step lies in identifying waste. In the realm of Kaizen, waste is classified into seven categories, broadly speaking: waiting, transport, motion, overproduction, over-processing, inventory, and defects. Each type of waste is prevalent in our daily lives at some level. For example, aimless scrolling on social media (motion), cooking more food than required (overproduction), or procrastination (waiting). Apply this lens to your daily life and work, assessing where wastage might occur. Journal your activities over a week, making note of tasks that consume considerable time or resources but bring scant value.

The next step is to devise strategies that gradually eliminate these wastes. Don't aim for a drastic overhaul; remember, the core of Kaizen is small continuous improvements.
Incorporate tools and techniques that enhance efficiency. For instance, apply the 2-Minute Rule to manage small tasks instantly rather than letting them pile up. Or use the Eisenhower Box to decide whether a task is worth your time and energy.

Habits also play a key role in averting waste. For instance, a daily routine where chores are assigned specific time slots aids in curbing procrastination (waiting) and aids in better work management (over-processing). Developing a habit of purposeful social media use prevents unlimited scrolling (motion), and planned meals avoid over-cooking or waste (overproduction).

Eliminating waste is a balancing act. It's about aligning your actions more closely with your goals and values, thereby creating more time and space for things that truly matter. Waste elimination is not about every minute being productive or busy. It's about ensuring time and energy are dedicated to tasks that really bring value.

Remember, pruning away the unnecessary gives life to the essential. By recognizing and eliminating waste, you're embracing the Kaizen philosophy. You're making room for productivity, efficiency, and, most importantly, your personal and professional growth. The process may sometimes feel slow, even painstaking, but it's a journey, and every step forward, no matter how small, is bringing you closer to a mindful existence—efficient, productive, and fulfilling. That's the profound power of Kaizen.

Streamlining Processes for Better Results

Streamlining processes—not merely for increasing efficiency but for enhancing overall output—is another facet of Kaizen. The idea may appear overtly corporate or industrial on the surface, but in reality, it can be applied judiciously across various spheres of our lives—personal, professional, even recreational.

Start by identifying the processes you engage in regularly—preparing a meal, writing a report, cleaning your house, preparing for a meeting. Each of these activities involves a process, a series of steps undertaken to achieve a specific outcome.

Next, audit these processes. Just as you did for waste identification, maintain a journal, noting down the details of these processes. For each process, outline each step you take, the time it consumes, the resources involved, and any challenges experienced.

Once the audit is completed, you're poised to begin the streamlining—eliminating unnecessary steps, optimizing resources, and resolving challenges. Kaizen would suggest starting with minor modifications rather than a complete makeover. Keep in mind that the objective of streamlining is not to reduce effort but to enhance output—making the processes as effective as possible.

Various tactics can assist in this objective. For instance, the implementation of checklists can help assure that no crucial steps are missed out, and the process flow remains smooth. Using efficient tools or platforms can expedite tasks and allow for more accurate results. Standardizing processes can reduce errors and enhance the quality of output.

Regular self-reflection pairs well with the streamlining process. Continuously reviewing and reflecting on your processes, successes, and challenges create a feedback loop that further refines your actions and leads to better results.

For example, if the process in question is meal prepping for the week, you could start by reducing the variety of meals to simplify shopping and cooking processes, using efficient tools like slow cookers to reduce active cooking time, and regularly reflecting on what works and what doesn't to make necessary alterations.

Streamlining processes, large or small, brings the essence of Kaizen to the forefront—continuous incremental improvements leading to better results. Enhancing the effectiveness of your processes means not only achieving what you aim for but doing so with less stress, less chaos, and a higher success rate.

By optimizing your daily processes, you're not just increasing your productivity but enhancing the quality of your output—and your life. With less time and energy spent on unnecessary or inefficient steps, you free up resources—for goals that really matter, for activities you truly enjoy. And that's the true essence of Kaizen—not just achieving more, but enhancing the quality of your achievements, your life, and ultimately, your happiness. Questa filosofia è un ciclo di miglioramenti continui e, a ogni giro, si progredisce verso il meglio: processi migliori, risultati migliori e una persona migliore.

Success Stories
of Efficiency Improvement

Witnessing the transformative power of Kaizen in real-life scenarios is truly inspiring. We have explored how progressive improvement techniques can enhance productivity, but how can they revolutionize our path to efficiency? We examine some success stories that reveal their full potential.

Consider the story of Rosa, a busy corporate executive who always had an obsession for books but struggled to find time to read. She decided to take the Kaizen approach and committed to reading 10 pages a day. She streamlined her routine, integrating this new habit into her existing schedule. Evenings, once spent aimlessly browsing the internet, were now devoted to her passion for reading. A year later, not only had she read over twenty books, but the habit of reading had improved her analytical skills, increased her knowledge base, and provided a regular means of unwinding from work stress.

Then, there's Mike, an entrepreneur, who constantly grappled with managing his company's operations. He applied the principles of Kaizen to identify different time-wasting activities that were hampering his productivity. He pinpointed excessive email checking as one critical area. He devised and implemented a new strategy—designating specific times during the day for email checking and responses. Slowly but surely, he began to regain control of his time, improving efficiency, and increasing his focus on core business activities.

Let's consider a non-professional scenario. Emily, a working mother of two, struggled with keeping her home organized. Instead of a significant overhaul, she opted for gradual changes, Kaizen style. She divided her home into different zones and committed to dedicating just 15 minutes per day to one particular zone. The task seemed small and achievable. Soon, it became a part of her daily routine. Six months later, her home was well-organized and easy to maintain.

Each of these examples highlights the importance of incremental and steady progress underscored by the approach based on small but continuous improvements. Overwhelm from too many changes at once was replaced by confidence as they consistently made small changes leading to significant improvements. They refined their processes, enhanced their efficiency, and reclaimed control over their time, each in their own domains.

These stories of efficiency improvement reflect that

enhancements in our personal and professional lives do not necessarily require dramatic, swift changes. On the contrary, small, intentional, and persistent steps can lead to profound transformations. It supports the notion that efficiency is not just about doing more in less time, but about focusing on tasks that bring the most value, thereby enriching our lives in the process.

As we journey through life, let's remember that the road to improvement, whether personal or professional, needn't be paved with huge leaps or radical shifts. Instead, it can be traveled with small, steady steps leading us to the ultimate destination— a more efficient, more productive, and more fulfilling life. That's the beauty and power of Kaizen, one small step at a time.

Implementing Kaizen at Home and Work

Applying the principle of progressive improvement in both the work and personal contexts can generate an environment characterized by steady growth and progress.

In a work setting, Kaizen can influence many aspects. Start by identifying repetitive tasks. What can be done to make these processes more efficient? Can they be automated, or would implementing certain tools help minimize time and effort? Next, target areas of waste. Are there tasks that consume significant resources but don't deliver equivalent value? Can these tasks be eliminated or modified?

Don't ignore the value of regular reflection. Make it a habit to review your accomplishments, identify the challenges faced and the lessons learned. This simple habit of retrospection can lead to better decision-making, thus refining your work methodologies and increasing efficiency over time. An atmosphere of constant learning and growth can significantly boost team morale and foster a culture of mutual development. Applying Kaizen at home involves a similar approach. Small improvements in housekeeping, meal prep routine, even financial management can make significant impacts. For example, spending a few minutes each night to plan the next day's activities or meals can lead to smoother mornings and less chaos. An important aspect of implementing Kaizen at home is to involve all family members. Fostering a sense of shared responsibility can create a harmonious living environment where everybody contributes to the overall well-being of the household.

Whether in the work or home context, the continuous improvement approach invites a transformation in thinking: from "it is good enough" to "it can be even better." It involves accepting the idea that there is always room for refinement, that no process is so flawless that it cannot be refined further.

It is important to remember that although the idea behind it is intuitive, adopting this philosophy involves a significant mental revolution: the belief that improvement is always possible and desirable, that taking small, consistent steps is valuable, and that success often lies not in prodigious leaps, but in the constant striving to surpass oneself day by day. By understanding and adopting Kaizen, you not only become an agent of change but also a harbinger of growth, perpetuating a cycle of constant improvement, both personally and professionally. The essence of the progressive improvement approach is beautifully summarized in this quote by Robert Collier: "*Success is the sum of small efforts, repeated day after day.*"

Kaizen embodies this very spirit of success—one small step at a time, every day, leading to a perpetual journey of growth, efficiency, and satisfaction.

Overcoming Obstacles with Kaizen

Identifying and Addressing Challenges

The journey towards personal and professional growth is rarely a direct path. It meanders, often encountering obstacles along the way. Kaizen philosophy can significantly assist you in navigating these challenges, turning them into opportunities for learning and growth.

The first step in our journey of overcoming obstacles is identifying the challenges. They could be external—like workplace dynamics and market trends—or internal, such as procrastination, fear of failure, or lack of focus. Recognizing our hurdles is the first stride we take towards overcoming them.

To illustrate this process, we'll use a commonplace challenge many of us face—procrastination. The first step towards tackling this obstacle would be acknowledging it—understanding that putting things off indefinitely is hindering your potential to grow and excel. Once you've identified the problem, the next part of your journey is to take small steps to mitigate it. Kaizen trains us to realize that change doesn't need to be daunting or overwhelming. It teaches us the power of small, consistent steps in inducing significant transformations.

With procrastination, implementing the '2-minute rule' can be an excellent place to start—ensure that tasks which take two minutes or less are done right away. You can take this a notch higher by slightly stretching the boundaries—expand the '2-minute rule' to a '5-minute rule. However, addressing challenges isn't always about personal willpower and motivation; it often requires systematic changes. Once again, Kaizen can guide us here. An examination of our typical routines can often spotlight areas of improvement. For instance, limiting distractions in your workspace can help combat procrastination, leading to more 'focused work' periods.

The Kaizen approach makes overcoming hurdles less intimidating, translating substantial challenges into manageable tasks. It allows us to gradually chip away at our problems without feeling overwhelmed. Maintaining a journal of your journey can be immensely helpful. It keeps track of your progress, offering clear visibility of the steps you have taken, the challenges encountered, and how you've tackled them. It serves as your personal roadmap, an evidence of your perseverance, and a wellspring of motivation when the going gets tough.

Remember, Kaizen is not about quick-fix solutions; it's about lifelong improvement. It's not simply about overcoming challenges, but about evolving through them. It's in these seemingly tough spots that we find opportunities to grow, to improve, to unleash our potential. By continually identifying and addressing our challenges, we position ourselves on a path of growth and self-improvement—a path that Kaizen lights for us, one small step at a time.

Kaizen Approach to Problem Solving

The Kaizen approach to problem-solving is characterized by its simplicity, accessibility, and emphasis on continuous improvement. It entails identifying problems and their root causes, finding solutions, implementing changes incrementally, and then continually monitoring these changes.

Think of problem-solving as sailing a boat. You notice the boat is drifting off course. Instead of panicking and making a sharp turn, which could tip the boat over, you make gradual adjustments, continually checking your path and adjusting your course until you reach your destination. That is the essence of the Kaizen approach to problem-solving.

Let's delve into how this approach can be used in practical settings. Suppose you're a project manager, and you've noticed the quality of work delivered by your team has been declining. Instead of hastily throwing together an all-embracing overhaul of your project procedures, you opt for the Kaizen approach.

Start by identifying the problem – declining work quality. Document specifics about the performance issues. Next, dig deeper to understand the root cause. Perhaps it's due to unrealistic deadlines, poor communication, or lack of skill training. Each cause would warrant a different solution, and identifying the correct cause is pivotal for resolving the issue.

Once the cause is identified, think of possible solutions. If unrealistic deadlines were the problem, could you adjust timelines? If it's a communication issue, perhaps regular check-ins could help. If it's a skills gap, maybe a training session is required.
Now it's time to implement these solutions – remember, make small changes. Begin with adjusting one project's timeline or initiating weekly check-ins for one team or conducting one training session. This gradual implementation reduces resistance to change and makes the adaptation process smoother. Once the changes are in effect, it's time for constant monitoring. Are the adjustments working? Has the work quality improved? The monitoring phase is crucial because it helps gauge the efficacy of the change and provides insights for future problem-solving.

The Kaizen approach to problem-solving can be a transformative strategy for individuals and organizations alike. When faced with a problem, we often seek quick fixes or drastic changes hoping that they'll rectify the situation. The continuous evolution approach perceives problems not only as challenges to be overcome, but as real opportunities to evolve and progress.
In a world that often idolizes big leaps and rapid transformations, Kaizen reminds us of the real power of small, continuous changes. When it comes to problem-solving, remember that it's often the

incremental changes that smoothly steer the boat to its destination. Kaizen's approach to problem-solving is a testament to its philosophy: Big improvements are a result of many tiny improvements adding up over time.

- Maintaining Motivation and Focus

Maintaining motivation and focus is vital for achieving goals and consistently improving, but these are areas where many of us struggle. However, the goodwill of Kaizen philosophy shines here effectively.

The most encouraging element of the small-step approach is its emphasis on discrete and easily manageable changes. This methodology transforms goals that may seem daunting into smaller tasks that do not require excessive motivational commitment or concentration.

Want to start a fitness regimen but struggling with motivation? Start with five minutes of activity a day. Seeking to write a book but can't find focus? Aim to write one paragraph every day. The tasks are easy, the commitment is minimal, yet the progress, over time, can be substantial.

Maintaining focus can often be tricky in a world brimming with distractions. Kaizen can be instrumental here as well. Begin by identifying your distractions, pinpoint those activities that are eating up your time but not adding substantial value. Once identified, devise tiny steps to eliminate or reduce these distractions. Perhaps you could start by designating a "no phone" time each day or unsubscribing from unnecessary email newsletters.

Kaizen also highlights the importance of a conducive environment for maintaining focus. Your surroundings play an essential role in your ability to focus. Is your workspace clutter-free and organised? Could adding a plant or some soft music enhance your concentration? Remember, tiny environmental tweaks can lead to significant improvements in focus.

Motivation, often mercurial, would find a stable ally in Kaizen. Nature of small changes is such that they require minimal motivation but lead to vast achievements over time, fuelling further motivation. Observing tangible progress serves as a powerful stimulus: in fact, one of the central pillars of the step-by-step improvement approach is confidence in the power of continuous small positive steps forward.
Keeping track of your progress also acts as an effective motivator. Consider maintaining a journal highlighting your journey, the small steps you're taking, and the progress you're making. Over time, this journal will serve as visual evidence of your growth, propelling your motivation.

Finally, Kaizen teaches us to appreciate the present moment and understand that improvement is a journey, not a destination. Focus on the task at hand, no matter how small. Dedicate yourself to the present moment, immerse in it, and the worries of the past and the future would fade into insignificance, leaving you with heightened focus and motivation.

Whether personal or professional goals, Kaizen offers a practical, effective approach to maintaining motivation and focus. It distils the vastness of ambition into trickles of daily tasks—an approach that not only paves the path to success but broadens the realms of what we consider achievable. When harmonized with the foundation of incremental development, motivation and focus are no longer obstacles but become launching pads to success.

One small step after another.

Learning from Failure:
A Kaizen Perspective

At the heart of the Kaizen philosophy lies the acceptance and understanding of failure as an integral part of growth and improvement process. Physically and mentally challenging to endure, failures can shake our confidence and deplete our motivation. However, incremental development brings with it the realization that failures, if constructively interpreted, can become strong stimuli for radical transformations and the achievement of success.

Learning from failure begins with accepting that setbacks are not a testament to your inability, but stepping stones toward improvement and knowledge. They are a sign you have dared to push your boundaries and try. The stigma associated with failures often overshadows this powerful insight.

Kaizen encourages us to shift our perception of failure—reshaping it from a dead-end to a detour towards the right path. Only when we have accepted failure as an opportunity to learn can we glean insights from it. Let's consider an example. A saleswoman consistently fails to meet her monthly targets. Instead of being disheartened by the failure, she applies Kaizen to reframe her perspective. She begins by identifying the areas where she fell short—was it poor lead generation, lack of follow-ups, or ineffective presentation skills? She analyzes her 'failure,' step by step, understanding and jotting down what went wrong.

Once the shortcomings are identified, she then

focuses on individual points, one at a time, to start making small improvements. Perhaps she could begin by seeking feedback from clients, attending a workshop to refine her presentation skills, or setting reminders for timely follow-ups. The goal isn't to achieve an immediate turnaround in fortunes; it is to make incremental improvements that, over time, will culminate in a substantial enhancement of her sales performance.

Through this process, her failure becomes a motivator, a roadmap to improvement. What seemed like a setback morphs into an opportunity for growth and development. Of crucial importance in this process is persistence. Failure can often instigate the desire for swift and significant success. But Kaizen compels us to persist with small, continuous improvements. It encourages us to create a circle of constant growth–to keep learning, keep improving, keep persisting, irrespective of setbacks.

Constant refinement shows us that failure is not opposed to success, but is an element of it. Accepting failure, examining it and using the resulting knowledge to advance and develop represents the approach of constant refinement toward learning through mistakes.

Discarding the fear of failure and replacing it with a learning mindset progressively diminishes the pressure to avoid risks and encourages innovation and learning. Remember, it's okay to fail, it's okay to fall. What's crucial is that we rise each time we fall, making failure not our enemy, but our teacher. Through small, continuous learning from our failures, we journey towards success—a success built not despite failures but because of them. That's the essence of Kaizen, turning the 'has-beens' of yesterday into the 'can-bes' of tomorrow.

Action Plan
for Continuous Improvement

Creating an action plan rooted in Kaizen philosophy can be your compass towards steady improvement and success. It should embody the essence of incremental progress: small but steady, purposeful actions toward achieving one's goals. We begin by identifying our goal. Whether it is professional development, personal enrichment or honing one's skills, determine what you aspire to achieve. Incremental progress emphasizes goal clarity, so it is critical that your goal be precisely outlined. For example, instead of a generic "I want to read more," move toward a specific goal such as "I want to read 12 books this year."

Having a definite goal is just the first step. Kaizen urges you to break down this goal into mini-goals or tasks. Break down your yearly goal into quarterly, monthly, weekly, or even daily tasks, depending on the nature of your goal. So, if your target is to read 12 books this year, a monthly task would be to read one book a month, equating to reading approximately 30 minutes a day.

Your action plan must also include a method to monitor and review your progress. Regular reviews allow for course corrections where necessary, reinforce the motivation to persist, and provide perspective on your journey. You could maintain a journal to keep track of your progress, noting down your accomplishments, challenges faced, and the lessons learned on the way.

An essential aspect of your action plan must be to embrace the Kaizen philosophy throughout—patience and persistence. Do not expect overnight transformations. Change takes time, and real, sustainable change often comes through small, steady efforts. It's also crucial to note that your action plan isn't etched in stone. The inherent flexibility of continuous improvement allows, and even stimulates, adjustments in response to progress made, changes in context or evolving goals.

Ultimately, Kaizen isn't about rigidly adhering to a plan; it's about creating a lifestyle that values and strives for continuous growth and improvement. And this action plan is more than a roadmap to your goal; it's a testament to your commitment to continual self-improvement.

Remember, the journey of a thousand miles commences with a single step. Your Kaizen action plan invites you to take this step, then the next, and the next—guiding you patiently, persistently towards your destination. One small step after another, make the spirit of continuous improvement your own every step of the way.

.Hansei

反省

The Practice of Reflection:
Understanding Hansei

The Concept and Tradition of Hansei

As we proceed further in our journey towards self-improvement, we encounter another potent tool emerging from the land of the rising sun—Hansei. An integral part of Japanese culture, the practice of self-reflection goes beyond the simple self-analysis that its literal translation might suggest.

It is considered a fundamental component of Japanese cultural thought, representing marked humility and an intense aspiration for constant improvement. It is an introspective process where individuals turn their gaze inward, critically analyzing their actions and decisions, acknowledging their mistakes, and learning from them. Culturally, Hansei plays a significant part in Japanese tradition. It is believed that this practice has been shaped and cultivated by many centuries of Buddhist, Shinto, and Confucian teachings and philosophies. It derives from a deep-rooted societal value that views humility as an exemplary virtue. Through this practice of self-examination, people are encouraged to avoid conceit and arrogance, to critically examine their actions and decisions on a regular basis, and to maintain a receptive attitude toward refinement.

However, Hansei is not about self-deprecation or nurturing a sense of inadequacy. Instead, it encompasses accepting one's flaws and mistakes, recognizing them as opportunities for learning and growth. It promotes a mindset where personal development is a lifelong journey, a continuous process, rather than a destination. Importantly, This form of self-analysis is not limited to an investigation of the past, but has a forward-looking perspective, turning reflection into concrete actions for days to come. It motivates people not only to meditate on their past experiences, but also to implement the resulting insights into future initiatives.

Hansei is also viewed as a process of 'mental housekeeping.' By engaging in the process of self-reflection, individuals clear out unnecessary mental clutter, reevaluate their goals, and realign their actions towards those goals.

Hansei is a deeply transformative practice that goes beyond reflecting towards influencing behaviors and attitudes, encouraging continuous improvement, and fostering holistic personal growth. It nudges us, gently yet firmly, toward a path that, while it accepts and values our present self, also acknowledges our potential to evolve and advance.

As we explore Hansei's tradition, remember that it's not about remorse over our past mistakes; it's about using our past as a mirror reflecting insights and lessons that illuminate our path forward. It's an open invitation to pause, reflect, and grow, embodying the beautifully profound sentiment encapsulated in the words of Carl Jung, "Who looks outside, dreams; who looks inside, awakes." Dive into the deep well of self-reflection and awake to a newer, better you.

- The Role of Self-reflection in Personal Growth

Self-reflection, the central tenet of Hansei, plays a crucial role in personal growth. By indulging in regular periods of reflection, we embark on a journey of self-discovery, understanding our beliefs, values, behaviors, aspirations, and fears more deeply.
Engaging in self-reflection fosters emotional intelligence, enabling us to comprehend our emotions better, thereby managing them more effectively. Understanding why we react the way we do helps regulate our responses in future scenarios, enhancing our interactions with others and our overall emotional well-being.

Personal growth thrives on a nourishing bed of self-awareness. By probing the depths of our conscious and unconscious minds, self-reflection enhances self-awareness, giving us a more accurate understanding of our strengths, weaknesses, and individuality. Recognizing our abilities allows us to leverage them fully, while acknowledging our weaknesses gives us the opportunity to work on them and transform them into strengths.

Reflection also bolsters our decision-making skills. By offering valuable insights into our past decisions, it measures the gap between our intended and actual outcomes, helping us make more informed, considered choices in the future. The reflective process subsequently leads to far-sighted decision-making, minimizing the likelihood of future mistakes and regrets. Reflection contributes to our resilience, too. By reviewing our past challenges and hurdles, we grow to understand our coping mechanisms—and how to leverage them in the face of future adversity. It helps us identify our responses to stress and pressure, uncovering valuable information about our adaptability and resilience.

Moreover, self-reflection fosters a mindset of continuous learning and growth. It brings to forefront the idea that we are, and can always be, works in progress. In this age of constant changes and evolving standards, maintaining an open, learning mindset is indispensable for personal and professional development. Implementing self-reflection in your routine can also contribute to your goal-setting process. By reassessing your aspirations, future ambitions, and current direction, reflection can aid in setting smarter, more relevant, tangible, and meaningful goals aligned with your values and beliefs.

Fundamentally, self-reflection transforms us into more mindful individuals. It helps us live our lives more consciously, making deliberate choices rather than simply going with the flow. It guides us to be present in the moment instead of being lost in the past or anxious about the future.

Self-reflection, or Hansei, can be a transformative addition to your personal growth journey. In a world that often demands us to look outwards for affirmation and success, self-reflection gently nudges us to look inwards — inwards into our minds, our hearts, our values, our dreams — to find our path to growth lying waiting, ready to be discovered and traveled.

So let's pause, take a step back from our fast-paced lives, and indulge in the enlightening practice of Hansei. Gift yourself the time and space for reflection, and watch as your personal growth journey unfolds and flourishes in surprising and rewarding ways, one step at a time, one day at a time. After all, personal growth isn't a race but a journey—a journey best traveled with reflection as your trusted companion.

Incorporating Hansei into Your Routine

Incorporating Hansei into your daily routine enriches your personal and professional life with a clean slate for learning, growth, and immeasurable insights. The strength of this introspection lies in the ease with which it can be incorporated into your everyday routine. By making it an ongoing habit, deep self-analysis can become a persistent catalyst for your ongoing personal development. Simply begin by reserving a moment daily for reflection. For many people, the quiet hours of early morning or late evening may be conducive, while for some, an afternoon break could work. The key is to choose a period when you're least likely to be disturbed and can commit to with consistency.

Once you've decided on the timing, create a conducive environment for your Hansei session. You might prefer a tranquil space or enjoy the serenity of nature—perhaps a corner of your home, a park, or even your backyard. Wherever it is, it should be a place where your thoughts can roam free, devoid of disturbances or distractions.

Determine how you'll conduct your self-reflection. Some prefer simply pondering over their thoughts, while others might find writing an effective tool for capturing their reflections. Journaling allows for a more structured approach to reflection and provides a tangible record of your thoughts. Consider maintaining a Hansei journal to keep track of your insights, challenges, and growth.

The next step is to decide what to reflect upon. There's a spectrum of aspects you could explore: your beliefs, actions, reactions, emotional responses, interactions, accomplishments, setbacks, and much more. Initially, you might want to start with basic prompts such as 'what did I do well today?' or 'what could I have done better?' or 'what did I learn today?' As you get into the practice, you can delve deeper into your reflections.

To make it practical, focus on actionable insights. Hansei isn't just about introspection; it's about utilizing these reflections to inform and influence your future actions. Finally, show utmost honesty during meditation sessions. It's essential to be truthful with yourself during these times of reflection. It's only when you confront the truth—no matter how uncomfortable or inconvenient—that you can expect to navigate the path of real growth and improvement.

Consistency is key. Incorporating Hansei into your lifestyle isn't about sporadic bursts of reflection but about sustained continuity. Just as repeated drops of water can cut through rock, continuous introspection sessions can, over time, shape and transform your life.
As you progress, you'll notice your perception towards failure, success, and growth evolving, your emotional intelligence heightening, your decision-making skills sharpening, and your journey towards self-improvement gaining momentum.

Keep in mind, there is no universal 'correct' or 'incorrect' approach to integrating introspection into your life; there's simply 'your' approach. And 'your' approach is the one that harmonizes with your personal values, life's pace, your unique experiences, and your emotional landscape.

So begin today, start small, stay consistent. Let this reflective practice illuminate your actions with insights, your journey with learning, and your life with radiant growth. Turn towards Hansei, for in its tranquil depths lie the secrets of genuine improvement, the joy of self-discovery, the strength of emotional intelligence, and the courage to be your best self. Begin your journey of deep self-analysis today, for it is by meditating on ourselves that we find the ability to shape ourselves and grow.

Reflective Practices
for Daily Life

Now that we have established the foundation for incorporating mindful introspection into our daily routines, let's look at some self-examination practices that we might consider in order to adapt them to our lives. These practices, infused with the essence of Hansei, can initiate a positive ripple effect across diverse aspects of our daily lives.

One simple, yet powerful, reflective practice includes beginning your day with a few minutes of quiet contemplation. Before the world awakens and the clamor of daily life begins, take a few tranquil moments to map out your day, reflecting on what you hope to achieve. A calm start to your day can positively influence the rest of it.

Another potent reflective practice is the 'End of Day Reflection.' As the day draws to a close, dedicate a few moments to reflect upon it. What were your triumphs? Did you encounter any obstacles? How did you react to those challenges? What could you have done better? Remember to acknowledge and appreciate the progress, however small it might be.

A weekly reflection session can prove beneficial for gauging your progress towards bigger objectives. Reflect on your past week. Have you inched closer to your goals? What hurdles did you overcome? What lessons did you glean? By reflecting on your week, you not only gain a keen perspective on your progress but also can plan your future weeks more effectively.

Learning from interactions is another significant reflective practice. After any significant interaction or meeting, reflect upon it. Did it go as per your expectations? Were you able to communicate effectively? By critically analyzing our interactions, we can improve our communication skills, emotional intelligence, and interpersonal relationships.

Practicing mindful reflection during your downtime can also be enlightening. During activities like walking, cycling, or even doing household chores, allow your thoughts to wander. Many creative ideas and insights emerge when your mind is relaxed and unfettered.

Lastly, remember that Hansei is not just about self-reflection but also about using those reflections to inform your future actions. Therefore, an effective reflective practice would including devising a plan of action based on your reflections. Map out the steps you'll take to improve and overcome your challenges, based on the insights gleaned from your reflections.

As you journey through your day, remember to pause and reflect. Not just on your actions and decisions but also on your thoughts and emotions. Let Hansei be your guiding light in the bustling labyrinth of life, illuminating your path with insights, bringing clarity with its radiance, and cultivating growth with its warmth. As you incorporate these reflective practices into your daily life, remember that self-reflection is an art—the art of looking within, appreciating what lies there, and using that appreciation to nourish and shape your life. The canvas is your life, and you hold the brush. With every reflection, every stroke, paint your masterpiece. One reflection at a time, one day at a time, let the art of self-reflection transform you into the artisan of your life.

For many of us, the journey into self-reflection may seem daunting at first. We may be unsure of how to start or struggle with maintaining focus. In such situations, guided Hansei sessions can prove beneficial. These sessions, often led by a trained facilitator or following a structured guideline, can lead us gently into the realms of reflective thinking.

A guided Hansei session generally begins with establishing a serene, distraction-free environment. This ambiance helps stimulate an introspective state of mind. The facilitator then guides you to focus on your thoughts, actions, interactions, or decisions needing reflection.

Guided sessions might incorporate a range of techniques to aid the reflective process. This could include visualization exercises, prompted journaling, mindfulness exercises, or even reflective questioning.

A significant advantage of guided sessions is the structured approach they provide. They start with curating a focus for your session, posing targeted questions, and guiding you through the process of reflection. Progressively, they lead you to explore the depths of your thoughts and feelings, unravel your actions and reactions, and understand their implications. They help you identify patterns in your behavior, beliefs, and values. Effectively, they offer a secure structure within which you can freely explore the landscape of your thoughts.

Furthermore, these sessions also guide you in translating your reflections into actionable insights. Through structured questioning, they help you derive practical steps for improvement based on your reflections. They inspire you to not only indulge in self-reflection but also to utilize the gleaned insights to inform your future decisions.

Guided Hansei sessions can be particularly useful for individuals new to the practice of self-reflection. They offer gentle nudges down the path of introspection, providing support and direction as you venture into the enlightening voyage of self-discovery.
Over time, as self-confidence and deepening understanding increase, these guided sessions can become the starting point for an independent exploration of conscious introspection. They can be the guiding hand that initially steadies you, gradually empowering you to traverse your path of self-reflection independently and confidently. The road into the world of self-reflection might be new and unfamiliar, but remember—everyone has to start somewhere. So whether you are timidly stepping onto this path or are already a seasoned traveler, guided Hansei sessions can provide a beneficial framework to your journey towards self-discovery, growth, and improvement.

As you embark on this path, remember the words of Socrates—"An unexamined life is not worth living." So let us dare to examine ourselves, our thoughts, our actions. Let us dare to reflect and, through this reflection, dare to grow, to improve, to transform. One thought, one reflection, and one guided session at a time.

Hansei for Personal and Professional Development

Using Hansei to Enhance Career Aspirations

Hansei, with its potential for fostering self-awareness and continuous growth, can be a powerful tool in enhancing our career aspirations. The reflective insights gleaned from this practice can influence our career trajectory and progression significantly. Let's examine how to apply self-analysis to promote our professional development.

To begin, consider regularly reflecting on your career goals and aspirations through self-analysis. This exercise can help you check whether your actions are actually in line with your goals. It also provides an opportunity to review these goals, ensuring that they are in harmony with your skills, interests and principles.

In addition, conscious introspection can prove to be a useful tool for identifying and enhancing your core competencies and skills. By reflecting on your strengths and weaknesses, you can better understand your professional capabilities, learning to further leverage your strengths while recognizing areas needing improvement.

Applied consistently, Hansei can enable you to identify patterns in your work performance. Reflect upon your successes and setbacks. What factors contributed to your victories? Where did you stumble? Such analysis can unveil underlying patterns that can inform your future actions, enabling you to amplify your successes and minimize your mistakes.

Conscious introspection can also serve as a guide for your professional evolution and progress. Reflection on your professional journey imparts clear-eyed perspective on areas where further learning or skill enhancement might be beneficial. It can support your decisions about professional development and learning initiatives, up-skilling endeavors, or even potential career transitions.

The performance reviews and feedback you receive at work can also be substantial material for Hansei.

Instead of simply accepting these reviews, delve deeper. Reflect on them and draw out meaningful, actionable insights. Feedback, both praise and criticism, can serve as constructive input for your professional development—if reflected upon with an open, learning attitude.

In addition, self-analysis can promote keen emotional intelligence, an aspect highly valued in the working world. Taking the time to reflect on one's emotions, reactions, and behaviors in the work environment can enhance self-awareness on an emotional level, the ability to manage one's emotions, and interpersonal skills, thereby improving leadership skills and the quality of professional interactions.

Use self-analysis to navigate career transitions or critical decision-making moments. At turning points, weighing in on past experiences, successes, lessons learned, and desires can guide your decisions toward paths that reflect your professional goals and personal values.

Integrating Hansei within your professional sphere is about continually striving for improvement and evolution. It's about consciously steering your career path rather than merely being a passenger. It's about transforming the unintended brushstrokes of your career into deliberate strokes evidently bearing your signature. As you weave Hansei into your professional life, remember that it's not just about professional growth and progression. It's about personal evolution that inadvertently influences professional development. It's about refining not just your skills, but your perspectives, reactions, and approaches.

So embrace the invitation to self-analysis and

navigate the paths of your professional development not as a path strewn with pitfalls, but as a conscious march. Within you resides immense potential for constant refinement and transformative growth, all rooted in your focused reflections, your intentional awareness, your practice of conscious introspection. Start today, reflect, and step closer to your career aspirations one insight at a time.

Building Stronger Relationships Through Reflection

In the realm of personal relationships, whether with family, friends, or romantic partners, Hansei can manifest as a profound tool for growth and understanding. Reflective practices can unveil insights about our behavior, communication, emotional responses, and expectations in our relationships, thus contributing to their growth and stability.

One of the foundational aspects of a successful relationship lies in understanding and managing our emotions effectively, a facet honed through self-reflection. The greater our emotional awareness, the better equipped we are to navigate our responses in various relationship scenarios. We become more capable of expressing our feelings authentically and constructively, thereby enhancing our emotional connections. Hansei can also provide a platform to reflect upon our communication patterns. It offers a mirror to evaluate our spoken and unspoken communication. Regular reflection on our communication can illuminate areas where misunderstandings may arise, enabling us to refine and improve our skills over time.

Self-reflection also lends clarity to our expectations in relationships. This clarity helps to diffuse potential conflicts arising from unmet or unrealistic expectations. Through regular reflection, we can align our expectations with reality, leading to healthier, more balanced relationships.

Hansei can also aid in resolving conflicts and misunderstandings. Reflecting on conflicts, instead of merely reacting to them, can help us understand the underlying issues. We can take responsibility for our part, learn from these instances, and devise strategies to avoid recurring patterns of disagreement.

By reflecting on our relationships, we can better appreciate the strengths and imperfections of both ourselves and those we share relationships with. This acceptance, rooted in love and respect, can strengthen our bonds and foster deeper, more satisfying relationships. Hansei can guide us in our journey of forgiveness. Reflecting on past hurts and misunderstandings paves the way to heal and forgive. Through reflection, we often find the strength and wisdom to release old grudges, thereby creating space for growth and renewal in our relationships.

Remember that our relationships are constantly changing entities, which can blossom significantly under the beneficial effect of conscious introspection. By adopting this practice in our interactions, we outline a path toward conscious affectivity, empathic communication and balanced companionship. As we navigate the complex journey of human relationships, guided by self-analysis, we discover that the process is not only about growing alongside our loved ones, but also about maturing inwardly. Our emotional intelligence develops, our capacity for empathy broadens, and our way of loving becomes deeper.

So employ Hansei in building stronger, more fulfilling relationships. Step forward into a realm where reflection enhances understanding, love transcends imperfections, and every interaction becomes a stepping stone to growth. Remember, it's in understanding ourselves, we understand others better. With each reflection, build a bridge of love, communication, and understanding—one that withstands the tests of time and strife.

May your path in relationships, skillfully illuminated by deep reflection, turn into a story of love, understanding and personal evolution. And along this path, may you not only see your relationships in a different light, but also discover hidden aspects of yourself. This is the power of self-analysis. This is the power of introspection. Nurture it, protect it and observe how your relationships blossom through its influence.

The Impact of Hansei on Communication Skills

Communication—the art of expressing and exchanging thoughts, feelings, and ideas—is a cornerstone of our personal and professional lives. Like any art, it too is subject to refinement and enhancement. Here, Hansei enters as a silent enhancer, a reflective canvas that can foster improvement in our communication skills.

One of the key aspects in which conscious introspection enriches our communication is by promoting emotional sensitivity. Analyzing our emotional reactions to various stimuli helps us understand, control and express our feelings more effectively. By gaining awareness of our emotions, we are able to interact more empathetically and genuinely, thereby refining our interaction with others.

Self-analysis can also greatly sharpen our listening skills, a fundamental but often underestimated component of effective dialogue. By stimulating us to assess how we listen, it can reveal whether we are truly present in the conversation or just waiting for the moment to intervene. This reflection invites the practice of active listening, which requires complete attention, understanding and empathy, all of which elevate the quality of our communication.

Conflict resolution is another sphere where Hansei can prove valuable. Reflection upon our reactions to disagreement can provide insights into our conflict management styles. By understanding our default reactions and resolving to improve, we can approach future conflicts with wisdom, patience, and openness to resolution. Reflective practice also empowers us to become more articulate, helping us express our thoughts, ideas, and feelings more clearly and concisely. By continuously reflecting upon our verbal and non-verbal cues, we can gradually become more effective communicators.

Moreover, Hansei can enable us to enhance our assertiveness—a key to balanced communication. Regular reflection on our past interactions can help us understand if we tend toward passive, aggressive, or assertive communication. Realizing this can guide us towards adopting a more assertive style, fostering healthier, more respectful communications. Importantly, Conscious introspection strengthens our ability to offer and accept feedback constructively, a valuable skill in both personal life and in the work context. Reflective practice encourages us to perceive feedback not as criticism but as an opportunity for growth. Likewise, we learn to give feedback in a manner that respects and acknowledges the individual's feelings.

Remember, effective communication isn't just about speaking convincingly but also about listening actively, comprehending accurately, and responding empathetically. It's about creating an authentic connection that transcends the barriers of misunderstanding, indifference, and judgment. Such an enriching quality of communication doesn't come naturally to many but can surely be cultivated and refined through Hansei. When you adopt mindful introspection to refine your communication techniques, keep in mind that it is not only words that convey your thoughts. Feelings, intentions, bodily expressions and even moments of silence convey messages. Be mindful and meditate on this.

So let us begin our journey to improve our communication skills through self-analysis: one dialogue, one reflection, one perception at a time. Elevate your interactions to a level of genuine understanding, sharing of meaning and authentic connections. Harness the power of Hansei to transform not just the words you speak but the very essence of your communication.
In this endeavor, may you discover not just the power of effective communication, but also the strength of your voice, the depth of your empathy, and the expanse of your understanding. This is the power of conscious introspection: enhancing communication, revolutionizing relationships.

Case Studies: Transformation Through Hansei

To further cement our understanding of Hansei's transformative potential, let's navigate through a series of case studies. These are authentic examples of individuals who have skillfully applied self-analysis for their personal enrichment and professional advancement, recording substantial changes in their life path.

The first example concerns Maria, an executive in a large international company. She was recognized for her commitment and dedication, but she encountered difficulties in communicative assertiveness. She tended to oscillate between passive acceptance and aggressive opposition, without finding a balance. She decided to adopt mindful introspection in her daily life, pondering over her communication styles, emotional reactions and underlying feelings. Progressively, Mary developed greater assertiveness, learning to share her thoughts and opinions respectfully and effectively. This change led to marked improvement in her personal interactions and collaboration with the team.

Next is the journey of David, an entrepreneur challenged with managing his growing team and business expansion simultaneously. Amidst the increasing professional demands, David found himself overwhelmed and stressed. It was at this juncture he discovered Hansei. Initially, he used it to vent out his worries and frustrations, but slowly, the reflective practice transformed into a platform for clarity and strategic planning. David began assessing his leadership style, team dynamics, business module, and his holistic lifestyle. The resultant insights guided him to improvise, learn, delegate, and balance his professional and personal life.

Sandhya, an aspiring artist, forms our third case study. While she was creatively gifted, her fear of criticism and failure hampered her growth. Regular Hansei sessions allowed her to confront these fears and doubts. As Sandhya reflected on her fear of criticism, she realized it stemmed from a deep-seated fear of rejection. Self-analysis also transformed Sandhya's way of seeing, as she began to interpret criticism as opportunities for constructive feedback essential to her creative journey. This new vision motivated her to explore, produce, and exhibit her art with greater freedom and without fear.

Our last case study spotlights Amina, a university student struggling with focus and productivity. Procrastination was a constant hurdle, keeping her from reaching her full potential. Embarking on a Hansei journey, Amina reflected on her study patterns, distractions, stress levels, and aspirations. She started implementing small strategic changes. Shorter study durations, prioritized task lists, regular breaks, and self-rewards were some of the improvements Amina introduced into her study plan. Steadily, her productivity improved, academic performance soared, and importantly, she reported lower stress levels.

These examples clearly illustrate the transformative power of self-analysis in various areas of life. They show how conscious and regular reflection can promote personal and professional development, enrich relationships, sharpen communication skills, increase productivity, and provide the tools to deal with daily challenges.
Each person's path of introspection is distinctive,

shaped by their own struggles, contexts and goals. It is not the magnitude but the quality of change that makes the difference: the way one transforms, the lessons learned, and the progress made.

As you reflect on these transformations, remember, each one was a journey—one day, one reflection, one step closer to a better version of themselves. Yours can be too. Begin today—with Hansei, with reflection.

Reflective Exercises for Development

As we wrap up this chapter, let's introduce some actionable reflective exercises. Incorporating these into your routine can kick-start your Hansei journey, helping you cultivate a habit of self-reflection for personal and professional development.

One effective exercise involves maintaining a reflection journal. At the end of each day, dedicate some time to write about your day—your achievements, your encounters, your challenges, and your feelings. This process can prove highly enlightening, providing you insights into your daily life patterns.

Another practical exercise is the "Three Questions" technique. Simply ask yourself three questions at the end of each day or activity: What went well? What could have gone better? What will I do differently next time? This exercise encourages you to reflect on your successes and areas of improvement, and also prompts forward-thinking by considering future actions. Performing a weekly 'Life Audit' can be beneficial too. Set aside some reflective time each week to take stock of various areas of your life—relationships, career, personal growth, health, and hobbies. This exercise encourages broader life reflection and strategic planning for improvements.

You can indulge in reflection during 'quiet moments' as well. Everyday activities—like taking a walk, gardening, or simply having a quiet cup of coffee—can become opportunities for reflection. Use these moments to let your thoughts wander, reflecting on your life, dreams, values, or behaviors.

Last but not least, make 'Hansei Meetings' a part of your professional routine. These could be solitary sessions or team-focused ones, involving reflective discussions about projects, decisions, or general work performance and dynamics. This practice can foster an environment of learning and continuous improvement in the workplace. Remember, self-reflection, like any skill, requires practice. Initially, you might find it challenging; perhaps even confronting your own thoughts, feelings, and actions might feel uncomfortable. However, the more you immerse yourself in reflective practices, the more natural it will become, and the more profound your insights will grow.

As you begin this journey of introspection, keep in mind that your experience with Hansei is distinctly personal—contemplate what matters most to you, absorb knowledge in a manner that suits you, and allow yourself to develop at a rate that feels right for you. Whether it's personal growth, career advancement, enhanced relationships, or overall life balance, Self-analysis can be the beacon that guides you toward the goals you wish to achieve. One idea, one meditation, one movement at a time: welcome the enriching path of conscious introspection.

Mastering Hansei for Long-term Success

Advanced Techniques in Hansei

The beauty of Hansei lies not just in its simplicity but its potential for deepening. As your skills and familiarity with introspection increase, you may feel ready to probe more complex methods of deepening your practice of self-analysis. While this initially focuses primarily on a retrospective of events, ideas and actions, advanced introspection broadens its scope to preventive contemplation.

Anticipatory reflection is the practice of reflecting before action. It involves considering different scenarios, potential actions, and their likely repercussions. Such a preventive meditation approach helps to improve decision making, making it more informed and consistent with our principles and aspirations. Simulation of future scenarios becomes a key element of proactive introspection.
Visualize hypothetical situations and reflect on your potential responses, decisions, emotional reactions, and the possible outcomes of your actions. Meditative reflection adds another layer to your Hansei practice. Simply sit in a quiet space, focusing on your breath, letting your mind settle. As your mind enters a tranquil state, gently introduce reflective questions or thoughts. This fusion of reflection and meditation can significantly enhance your insight and self-awareness.

Paired reflections or reflective dialogues can be another enriching addition to your Hansei practice. Engage in reflective discussions with a trusted friend, partner, or mentor. These dialogues offer multiple perspectives, encouraging deeper understanding and enhanced personal growth.
'Sense writing' is another advanced technique, particularly beneficial for those with a creative inclination. This involves describing a memory using sensory details—what you saw, heard, smelled, tasted, or felt. This can facilitate greater recall leading to more in-depth reflections.

Lastly, 'solution-focused reflection' distinguished by

its goal-oriented approach, can enhance your development. Rather than focusing solely on problems, this type of reflection focuses on potential solutions and requisite actions for improvement.

Regardless of the strategy you adopt, the pillars of mindful introspection remain unchanged: acting with intentionality, sincerity, courage and openness to learning and personal development. Opt for the practice that best reflects your needs and experiment with different methods to broaden and vary your personal reflection.

Deepening self-analysis does not focus on intricate methodologies, but rather on a more intense connection with your own thoughts, feelings and behaviors. In approaching these advanced practices, it is crucial to remember that introspection does not follow a predefined path, but develops through a personal and dynamic journey that is as unique as the one who travels it. Therefore, continue to investigate, meditate and evolve. Immersed in self-analysis, you will discover a universe of genuine self-awareness, learning, refinement and change, step by step, reflection by reflection. This is the power of Hansei; this is the power of you. Nurture it, harness it, and soar towards continued personal and professional growth.

Creating a Sustainable
Practice of Reflection

A key facet of reaping Hansei's long-term benefits involves developing a sustainable practice of reflection. Establishing a habit of constant reflection ensures that the insights gained through conscious introspection will materialize in steady personal as well as professional development. Here, let's unravel the steps towards creating such a sustainable reflective routine.

One of the most significant factors influencing the sustainability of your Hansei practice is its seamless integration into your daily life. To start with, establish a specific time for reflection in your daily schedule. It could be in the morning, providing direction to your day, or at night, serving as a reflective recap of the day.

Next, choose a method that tantalizes your reflective leanings. If you're a writer, a journal might be the platform to pour your reflections upon. On the other hand, if you resonate more with verbal expression, consider voice recordings or reflective dialogues. The medium of reflection is less critical than the act itself; select a way that meshes smoothly with your preferences. Ensure that your reflective space is free from distractions. It could be a quiet corner of your home, your office, or even a natural setting if you prefer the outdoors. This space should foster tranquility, allowing your reflections to flow uninterrupted.

Setting thoughtful goals can also nurture your dedication to self-analysis. These might include weekly themes to reflect upon, specific developmental goals you hope to attain through Hansei, or an exploration into your past experiences or future aspirations.
Initially, regular reflection may seem tedious or even challenging, especially if you're acquainting yourself with your thoughts and emotions more closely. It's okay, the initial discomfort ebb away as you nurture your practice.

Moreover, avoid the trap of 'reflection perfectionism.' Your reflections don't need to be profound each day, nor do they need to unearth significant insights every time. Whether seemingly mundane or susceptible, it's your honesty and commitment to the process that counts. Celebrate your Hansei journey. Acknowledge the insights you gain, the growth you experience, and the positive changes you make. Recognizing these milestones can motivate you to uphold your reflective habit.

Creating a sustainable reflection routine, like any habit, demands time, patience, and consistency. It's a journey, not a destination—one, that promises a wholesome blend of self-awareness, growth, and transformation. As you commence on this path, remember that each day offers a new insight, a fresh perspective, a latent potential ready to blossom under your reflective gaze. So, savour this journey. Cultivate it one day at a time, one reflection at a time. Nurture your Hansei habit and let it guide you towards a life of continuous learning, growth, and personal success.

The Future of Hansei in Your Life

As we tread further along this path of self-reflection, let's envision the future of Hansei in your life. Visualizing its role in your forthcoming journey can provide direction, keeping you rooted in this transformative practice. Visualize a path in which every action taken, every choice made, is imbued with the depth of conscious introspection.

A path where reflection provides a roadmap to your deepest desires and loftiest objectives. Where it guides you to align your actions with your core values, leading to a synchrony between your pursuits and your principles.

Visualize a future where Hansei paves the way for improved relationships—ones marked by empathy, understanding, and authentic communication. A future where expressions bear the hallmarks of your reflective journey, embodying authenticity, empathy, and wisdom. A world where connections deepen, not just on a superficial level, but at a core human level, embracing imperfections, nuance, and diversity.

On your path to self-development, conscious introspection becomes a perennial ally, stimulating you to probe your capabilities and push your personal boundaries. It ignites a constant thirst for knowledge, fomenting an endless passion for learning. As you become more open to feedback and more open to development, it activates an upward spiral of constant refinement that guides both your personal and professional evolution.

Through self-analysis, the horizon of your professional possibilities also expands. A future awaits you in which your career is enhanced by perceptions, decisions and tactics inspired by reflection. Resistance to change subsides, as every change is seen as an opportunity to learn and grow. The very essence of your leadership also undergoes transformation, evolving from a directive stance to a reflective, empathetic approach. As a leader, you display more patience, more attention towards your team's growth, and importantly, a willingness to learn from them. Visualize a future where challenges no longer daunt you, but rather spark your reflective prowess. Each obstacle, setback, or failure becomes an opportunity for Hansei, guiding you towards creative solutions and enhanced resilience.

Finally, envision a future where the practice of Hansei impacts not just you, but the world around youWhen families, colleagues and communities integrate the principle of conscious introspection into their dynamics, we contribute to building a world enriched by empathy, mutual understanding and collective progress. Use the power of visualization to direct your path of self-analysis: imagine the effect, evolutions and possibilities it can bring. Let this image motivate you, orient you and encourage you to continue with determination in your practice of self-reflection.

This is a vision of a future steeped in self-analysis in your existence: a tomorrow characterized by growth, evolution, personal fulfillment and transformational successes.
A future led by reflection, punctuated by insights, and teeming with potential. Your future—where you are not just a passenger, but the driver, guided by the torch of Hansei.

Sharing the Practice of Hansei with Others

As Hansei enriches your life, you may feel called to share this transformative practice with others. Whether introducing the principle to colleagues, fostering introspective debates in the family or accompanying a friend on his or her journey of self-examination, popularizing conscious introspection extends its effect, generating a chain reaction of development and positive change in the context in which we live.

One way to promote self-analysis is through open

conversation. Initiate meaningful dialogues with friends, family members or colleagues about your experiences with self-analysis. Tell how self-reflection has sharpened your self-perception, optimized your choices and stimulated your personal advancement. Sharing your journey may bring them closer to the idea and motivate them to explore their own practice of introspection. Creating shared reflection spaces can foster a collective culture of self-reflection. Encourage group Hansei sessions within your family, peer group, or workplace—infusing reflective practices within group dynamics. These interactions can create a supportive environment for reflection, facilitating collective growth, understanding, and connection.

Proposing oneself as a reflective partner can be an effective way to spread the practice, especially among those who are less familiar with the concept. Through constant introspective conversations, this pair dynamic can foster mutual personal development, sharpen understanding and strengthen the relationship, promoting an environment of collective learning and growth. Consider making useful resources for self-analysis available to those who show interest. Their understanding of Hansei can be deepened by connecting them with literature, workshops, or even online forums dedicated to self-reflection. They might also appreciate insights into effective reflective exercises, aiding their initial exploration of self-reflection.

Leverage the potential of technology as a means of spreading mindful introspection. Blogs, podcasts, webinars, or social platforms can be effective in promoting the principle and reaching a wide audience. Highlighting the ease, accessibility and transformative effect of self-analysis can motivate others to explore this practice.

It is also helpful to encourage schools, universities and community centers to include self-examination in their curricula. Instilling an ethic of deep reflection from an early age can predispose new generations to develop a growth-oriented mindset, enhancing their capacity for learning, adaptability and resilience. Within the workplace, advocate for reflective professional development. Encouraging reflective leadership, team dynamics, and decision-making can foster a culture of continuous growth, innovation, and employee engagement.

In promoting the ethic of mindful introspection, keep in mind the principle of "reflect, not impose." By sharing your experiences, presenting the concept or providing applicable strategies, you allow recipients to decide how to incorporate this practice into their existence.

Through sharing Hansei, you do more than spreading a practice—you propagate a transformative philosophy. You inspire self-awareness, advocate empathy, and foster growth, not just on an individual level, but communal level—enriching relationships, interactions, and communities at large.

As you proceed to share Hansei, may you ignite curiosity, spark journeys of self-discovery, and contribute to cultivating a world where reflection thrives. Through dialogues, exchanges and shared meditations, we seek to make conscious introspection a journey of profound evolution for many. Therein lies the essence of self-analysis: transforming not only one's own life, but exerting an impact on multiple existences, one reflection after another.

As we reach the conclusion of this enriching journey through the realms of Hansei, it's crucial to underscore the essence of continuity. Meditation practice is not marked by final destinations, but is actually an ongoing journey, enriched by constant exploration, insight and growth.

It's a journey that is not always easy. There will be days when you'll face discomfort, resistance, even confusion. Thoughts and feelings you'd rather avoid might surface, and you might question the utility of retrospective treading. But it is in these moments that Hansei unveils its transformative prowess.

Every tough moment, every uncomfortable emotion, every challenging thought—these are not roadblocks but opportunities for deeper insight and growth. Amidst these turbulent times, recognize the power of patience, persistence, and compassion towards oneself. Cling onto your commitment to the process; embrace the complexities; let them guide you towards greater self-understanding. Never lose sight of your growth, however minute it might appear. It's there, intricately woven within your experiences, radiating in your newfound insights, marking subtle shifts in your thoughts, emotions, and actions. Celebrate this transformation; cherish your progress; let it fuel your Hansei journey.

As you venture further on this path of self-reflection, do take a moment now and then to look back, retracing your steps, basking in the glow of your growth. Observe the changes you've spawned, the wisdom you've acquired, the person you've become, and the potential you've yet to explore.

Continue on this path, allowing conscious introspection to instill in you a love of continuous learning, deep-rooted resilience, keen self-awareness, and solid confidence in your potential for development.

Remember, the true essence and value of self-analysis lies not in the time devoted to reflection, but in the honesty, receptivity and courage that flow from it. Whether you spend a minute or an hour, whether you glean an earth-shattering insight or a nuanced understanding of your thoughts, every bit counts, every moment matters in this journey.

The journey of Hansei, at its core, is but a voyage towards a deeper sense of self, a more profound connection with your values, emotions, and goals, and an enriched engagement with life. Let this journey continue to inspire, motivate, and transform your life—one reflection at a time, one day at a time. Here's to continuing the journey of reflection, of personal growth, of lifelong learning—here's to a future thrumming with the sounds of self-awareness, growth, and self-fulfillment. This is the essence of Hansei—a light to guide you, a path to tread, a journey to relish. Embrace it, cherish it, and let it guide you towards a life teeming with growth, fulfillment, and success.

Integrating Ikigai, Kaizen, and Hansei into Your Life

The Synergy of Ikigai, Kaizen, and Hansei for Holistic Success

As we arrive at our concluding chapter, let's revisit the powerful combination of Ikigai, Kaizen, and

Hansei for achieving holistic success in life. Together, these three form an enriching cycle of self-discovery, continuous improvement, and learning through reflection.

Ikigai, the exploration of your "reason for being," acts as the foundation of this cycle. It encourages self-discovery, guiding you towards what you love, what you excel at, what the world needs, and what you can be paid for. Your Ikigai serves as an internal compass, directing your actions, decisions, and long-term goals to align with your values, passions, and potentials. Once you've embarked on your journey of self-discovery, Kaizen steers the course, enabling you to pursue continuous improvements. Small, steady changes initiated under the Kaizen philosophy align your actions with your Ikigai, leading to progress and fulfilment. It's a patient, consistent methodology of goal achievement, emphasizing the potency of incremental progress.

The role of Hansei towers towards the end, yet equally integral, acting as the anchor of the cycle. As a practice, it encourages you to pause, reflect, and learn from your actions, bridging the gap between your Ikigai and Kaizen. Through conscious self-analysis, one gains perceptions about one's progress, areas that need development and future initiatives, thus facilitating thoughtful choices and relentless personal development.

The beauty of this synergy lies in its flexibility and adaptability. It's not about adhering to a strict set of rules, but rather embracing a flexible practice that shapes itself around your individual life experiences, ambitions, and journeys.

The integration of Ikigai, Kaizen, and Hansei creates

a self-sustaining cycle of aspiration, action, and review—a holistic roadmap to success. You begin with recognizing your Ikigai, chart your path with Kaizen, and ensure alignment through Hansei.

Imagine this as a three-pronged compass, helping you navigate life's journey. Ikigai points you to your destination, Kaizen walks you through the path, and Hansei ensures you're on the right track. The trio, while powerful individually, creates magic when working in unison. A life infused with the synergy of Ikigai, Kaizen, and Hansei is a life of purpose, productivity, learning, and continuous growth—a life of holistic success.

This is the essence of integrating Ikigai, Kaizen, and Hansei into your life—a true fusion of Japanese philosophies guiding your path to a fulfilled, balanced, and successful life. As you illuminate your path with this synergy, you not only strive for success but thrive in it-one step, one improvement, one reflection at a time. This interplay is your guide to a purposeful, productive, and rewarding life. Harness it, cultivate it, and stride towards the life you aspire to live. The magic of Ikigai, Kaizen, and Hansei awaits you—embrace it, cherish it, let it transform your world.

Strategies for Maintaining Balance and Continuous Growth

Given the fast-paced, often challenging world we live in, striking a balance between different life domains and maintaining continuous growth can indeed be a Herculean task. Integrating Ikigai, Kaizen, and Hansei into your daily routine equips you with effective strategies to navigate this balance and foster enduring growth.

Embracing your Ikigai aids you in creating an equilibrium in your life—balancing your passion, profession, vocation, and mission. To retain this balance, revisit your Ikigai regularly, realigning it to your evolving life circumstances, passions, and potentials.
While on this path, continue to seek out activities that align with your Ikigai. Whether it involves starting a new hobby, shifting to a more fulfilling career, or committing to lifelong learning—diligently follow what brings joy to your life and sparks your passion.

The Kaizen principle of continuous improvement lays the groundwork for maintaining steady growth in all areas of your life. It eschews complacency, advocating for consistent, incremental advancements. To uphold continuous growth, make Kaizen a part of your daily routine. Set small, manageable goals related to different aspects of your life—health, relationships, professional development, or personal pursuits. Consistently work towards these, embracing each small accomplishment as a step towards your long-term objectives.

Hansei, the practice of self-reflection, ensures that your balance and growth are well-aligned with your values and objectives. Regular reflective practices help maintain an awareness of your life's balance, alerting you when any aspect begins to tip disproportionately. Hansei fosters learning from experiences, equipping you to navigate challenges, reap growth from failures, and build resilience. Embrace Hansei as a catalyst for personal evolution, enabling you to adapt, overcome, and thrive amidst life's ebbs and flows.

Remember the importance of self-care in this journey of balance and growth. Amidst your pursuits, allow yourself moments of rest, joy, and rejuvenation—creating a healthy balance between striving for improvements and cherishing the present.

Lastly, be patient with yourself. Progression on the path of balanced living and continuous growth may at times be slow, replete with obstacles, detours, or even periods of stagnation. Such times are but natural elements of life's journey, spaces that often harbor the most profound growth and learning.
As you tread along this path, take pride in each small step, each incremental improvement, and every insightful reflection. Whether you're discovering your Ikigai, adopting a new Kaizen strategy, or delving into a deeper Hansei session, each action, each moment counts.

This pursuit of balance and unending growth is a journey—one filled with self-exploration, introspection, transformation, and above all, continuous learning. As you immerse yourself in this voyage, remember that the balance you seek is not a static state, but a dynamic harmony adapting to your evolving life conditions.

So, keep exploring your Ikigai, keep progressing with Kaizen, keep reflecting with Hansei. Let these Japanese philosophies paint your life canvas with rich hues of balance, growth, fulfillment, and success. Let them guide you in your quest for an enriching, purposeful, and thriving life—a life you love, a life you're proud of, and a life you're continually growing in. Herein lies the magic of integrating Ikigai, Kaizen, and Hansei into your life; embrace it and let it illuminate your path to holistic success and fulfillment.

Next Steps: Creating
Your Path Forward

Your journey forward, after this enriching stay with the Japanese triad, emerges as a unique path adorned with purpose, continual growth, and reflective wisdom. As we delve into creating this promising path, let's explore the steps that can guide you forward.

First, cultivate your Ikigai. Take your time to unravel your 'reason for being'
Find that congruent spot where your passion, career, calling, and life's mission converge—a place that reflects your values, vibrates with your enthusiasms, and leverages your capabilities. Remember, discovering your Ikigai is not an overnight quest but a lifelong journey of self-exploration. With the unveiling of each layer of your Ikigai, you create a clearer vision of your motivation, aspirations, and purpose.

Once you've unearthed the essence of your Ikigai, let Kaizen guide you in realizing it. Begin by setting specific, quantifiable, realistic goals aligned with your Ikigai. Break down bigger objectives into manageable smaller tasks—an approach that reduces overwhelm and keeps you motivated. Remember, the Kaizen philosophy places immense importance on small, consistent, incremental improvements. So, every small step forward, every tiny improvement, counts. Simultaneously, ensure to keep track of these small improvements. Maintain a journal, use an app or simply make a note of your progress. This practice helps you review your advancement, allowing you to

141

see, over time, how these tiny steps have contributed to significant growth.

Next, make Hansei—an integral part of your daily routine. Carve out time each day to reflect on your actions, decisions, achievements, and shortcomings. Use this time to not only contemplate your direction but also to celebrate your progress and absorb the lessons learned. Embrace your victories, understand your failures, and most importantly, be honest with the process.

As days turn into weeks, months, and years, continue building on your Ikigai, refining your Kaizen strategies, and deepening your Hansei practices. Your path forward is not a straight, pre-determined highway but a winding path, bending and curving as you manoeuvre through the terrain of life.

Along this journey, you may face obstacles, detours, and even dead-ends. Embrace them. They are not hindrances, but opportunities for growth and learning. Use your understanding of Ikigai to find purpose in these situations, apply Kaizen to overcome challenges, and resort to Hansei to derive wisdom from these experiences.

Don't fall into the trap of comparison—the pace, progress, and path will be different for each individual. Build your journey on your terms, at your pace, in alignment with your goals and values.

So here you stand, on the cusp of an exciting new beginning—a voyage shaped by the interplay of purpose, continuous improvement, and reflective wisdom. A journey where your purpose serves as your compass, the steady pace of improvement propels you forward, and the light of reflective wisdom guides your steps. What lies ahead is a path of self-exploration, consistent advancement, and insightful contemplation, strewn with challenges and celebrations, learning and achievements.

The fusion of the Japanese triad is in balance with its purpose, constantly improving, reflecting regularly, resulting in a fruitful existence.

As you create your path forward, let these philosophies illuminate your journey, guiding you towards a fulfilling and successful life. This is not the end, but the beginning of a profound journey—a voyage into uncharted territories of self-exploration, transformation, and life-long learning.

You're set to move ahead with assurance, holding the insights you've gathered close, and welcoming the life's journey that awaits—a path filled with boundless opportunities, glowing with the potential for true contentment, and rich with collective achievement.
With the wisdom we have gathered through studies of the Japonese triad, we now stand on the precipice of a remarkable journey dawning before us. A journey that promises to be an exploration of soul, self, and purpose. Yet, just as this path begins, it never ends—it unspools constantly before us, propelled by our unending quest for fulfillment and success. Each day is an opportunity for renewal, a new chapter in your life's narrative. One woven intricately with the threads of Ikigai, Kaizen, and Hansei—each philosophy enriching your life's tapestry with vivid hues of purpose, improvement, and reflection.

Anchor your days in the search for your Ikigai. It's an ongoing exploration transpiring in your daily decisions, choices, and actions—in the language you speak, the relationships you nurture, the career you pursue and the passions you kindle. Amidst life's routines, ensure you dedicate time to your Ikigai—cherishing what you love, honing what you are good at, catering to what the world needs, and transforming it into what you can be compensated for.

As your Ikigai leads your way, let Kaizen be your constant companion, reminding you of the transformative power within incremental progress. Wherever you are, whatever you do, the spirit of Kaizen can be employed. Whether it's breaking down a professional goal into small manageable tasks, developing a healthy habit, enhancing a relationship or mastering a hobby—one small step at a time, progress is always within reach with Kaizen.

Hansei, the practice of critical self-reflection, is your guiding star on this life's voyage, illuminating your path, revealing where you are and how far you have journeyed. Embrace Hansei whole-heartedly—learning from your past, acknowledging your victories as well as your failures, and using them as catalysts for self-improvement and growth.

The structuring of your story is in your hands—you are the author of your life, and these philosophies are tools for you to compose an enriching bestseller. Your life's narrative will have its highs and lows—it's sunshine and storms, but every episode, every scene contributes to the person you become. Every moment you devote to finding your Ikigai, every small improvement you make with Kaizen, every reflection you undertake with Hansei—these are not discrete, isolated incidents, but bricks in the construction of your stately dwelling called life.

While we conclude our discussions here, your journey with these profound Japanese philosophies continues. You are the warrior venturing into uncharted territories of self-awareness, growth, and lifelong learning – equipped with a robust compass guiding you towards fulfillment and success, Kaizen navigating you over obstacles and Hansei illuminating your path with insightful reflections.

As you take the helm steering your ship forward, embrace the winds of change, navigate through the azure waters of life, sometimes calm, sometimes choppy, let these philosophies keep you strong and guide you. Here's to a fulfilling, balanced, and successful future—one that's certainly within reach, with Japanese triad as your trustworthy companions. So, as we embark upon this new dawn, let us let the wisdom of Ikigai, Kaizen, and Hansei steer our lives towards a brighter horizon—one where purpose, continuous growth, and self-improvement form the triumphant axis of our existence. May the spirit of Ikigai light your passions, may Kaizen inspire you in your pursuits, and Hansei enrich your journey with insights and wisdom. Here's to a vibrant life—a beautiful voyage pulsating with the essence of triad.

As we approach the final stretch of our time together, let's revisit the essence of our journey—the diligent integration of triad into our lives. These philosophies offer profound wisdom, inadvertently becoming our compass, our guiding manual in the dynamic spectrum of life.

In our personal and professional lives, there may be times when the excitement, fulfillment, and purpose seem to fade, overwhelmed by the cacophony of life's demands. During such moments, the inspiring concept of Ikigai can be a beacon, helping to re-ignite our passion and guide us back to our core values and potential—towards our unique 'reason for being'.

As we progress in this encouraging cadence, we are invited to embrace the principle of continuous improvement—taking incremental steps toward our goals. This applies across the spectrum of life's endeavors, from developing a skill to strengthening relationships, from maintaining health to bettering our communication. Every sphere of life serves as fertile ground for this practice, where small yet positive shifts can gradually build and reinforce our life's framework, one step at a time.

On this path, you will find in meditation a trusted partner, not only as a principle but as a philosophy of life. An encounter with a problem, an unexpected situation or even a predictable routine: each one represents an opportunity for Hansei. So welcome these opportunities, take a pause from the journey and reflect—critically and honestly. Use these insightful moments to iterate your actions, improve your strategies, and define your future course.

In this vast tapestry of existence, the vibrant threads of life purpose, the steady progression of personal improvement, and the gentle patterns of introspection weave together to form a stunning pattern—one that echoes with meaning, persistent advancement, and thoughtful contemplation.
So, carry forward these philosophies with you—not as mere lessons, but as a new lens to gaze upon life, a compass that guides you through the maze of existence, and a driving force that propels you ahead. Apply, integrate, and resonate with them, and they will chart a life course for you, teeming with balanced success and fulfillment.

This journey that we embarked upon together has hopefully enriched you, empowered you with knowledge, and inspired you to transform and blossom into your best self. It's a new dawn filled with promise, and the arena is all set for you to step into and carve a niche for yourself.

Embrace Ikigai, welcome Kaizen, and embody Hansei—integrate them as everyday practices, as consistent life strategies. Let their wisdom permeate every facet of your existence, illuminating your path to a fulfilling, enriching, and triumphant life. Remember, you are on a journey of growth and learning, and with these philosophies to guide you, you are bound to thrive.

As we conclude this chapter, remember—every end is a new beginning. So here's to new beginnings—a beginning of wisdom, growth, fulfillment, a beginning of your journey with Japanese triad, and most importantly, a beginning of your relentless pursuit of a life of purpose, success, and unending growth. A thriving, fulfilling life is not a far-off dream but a reality within your grasp—embrace it! As we draw to the end of this exploration into Ikigai, Kaizen, and Hansei, I would like to extend my heartfelt gratitude for entrusting me with your journey of personal development and self-discovery. I am honored to have had the opportunity to share in this exploration, and I hope this journey has been as enlightening for you as it has been for me.

Together, we have traversed facets of life—plumbed its depths, scoured its expanse, and scaled its heights. We delved into discovering our Ikigai—the underlying purpose that can lend our existence vibrance and direction. We've come to grasp the nuanced steps of continual betterment through Kaizen, guiding our lives in a steady tempo toward our aspirations. We've also learned to value the deep calm that comes with moments of introspection, using Hansei to reassess and recalibrate the course of our life's journey.

The concepts of Ikigai, Kaizen, and Hansei, each powerful individually, form a compelling force when merged, a beacon to guide us on the path of personal and professional metamorphosis. It steers us, consistently, confidently towards a life of unceasing growth, defined purpose, and insightful reflection—a life enriched, a life fulfilling.

These Japanese philosophies do not propose quick fixes but favor gradual, sustainable changes leading to concrete, lasting results. And while each philosophy offers a unique perspective, together they create a comprehensive design for a meaningful and goal-oriented life. Cultivating your Ikigai, you brought clarity to your intrinsic motivations and unique talents—a clear vision of what stirs your soul, engages your skills, sets the world in need, and can ensure your financial stability. Embracing Kaizen, you seized the power in small, consistent changes—proving that progress doesn't always require monumental leaps. Every tiny step forward, every incremental improvement, is a victory, reinforcing your capabilities and boosting your confidence.

You've seen how patience, persistence, and small, steady advancements develop into significant transformations over time. Adopting Hansei fostered introspection and encouraged reflection on your choices, helping you learn from your successes and failures. This practice opened vistas for personal growth, equipping you to adapt from experience and make robust, informed decisions. Self-evaluation has become a constant, leading to a deeper understanding of your life's journey.

Bringing these philosophies together, you're now poised to weave a tapestry of holistic success—

directed by your Ikigai, sustained by Kaizen, and polished by Hansei.

This integration is your map to your deepest passions and loftiest dreams, guiding you through the plains of daily living into the altitudes of accomplishment. It infuses your journey with purpose, enriches it with continuous growth, and renews it with insightful reflections—a journey that, I hope, makes your life sweeter and more worthwhile. Our shared path is just the beginning. An immense field of learning, experimenting, and growth lies before you. With the insights of purpose, continuous improvement, and self-reflection, you are well-equipped to set sail on this exciting expedition—to navigate the breadth of opportunities, to overcome the highest of obstacles, to savor the victories, and to emerge stronger from the setbacks.

Every end merits a new beginning, and the conclusion of our time together is no different. It's the dawn of your journey forward—a journey marked by endless learning, continuous progress, insightful reflection, and immeasurable fulfillment.

I hope that this exploration has instilled in you a sense of purpose, resilience, and adaptability, inspiring you to create a fulfilling life teeming with growth, balance, and success. May the essence of Ikigai illuminate your path, the power of Kaizen propel you forward, and the spirit of Hansei enrich your journey.

Here's to your journey forward—beautiful, vibrant, and thrilling. Here's to you—embracing your Ikigai, exploring Kaizen, embodying Hansei. Here's to your fulfilled, vibrant, and successful life. The journey continues, and the possibilities are endless. Embrace them, explore the horizon and paint your masterpiece of life with the vibrant hues of Ikigai, Kaizen, and Hansei.

Printed in Great Britain
by Amazon

50546066R00086